Handling Conflict

Taking the Tension Out of Difficult Relationships

Gerry Rauch

SERVANT BOOKS
Ann Arbor, Michigan

Cover design by Charles Picirilli, Graphicus Corp.

Published by Servant Publications, P.O. Box 8617, Ann Arbor, Michigan 48107

ISBN 0-89283-187-1
Printed in the United States of America

85 86 87 88 89 10 9 8 7 6 5 4 3 2 1

Library of Congress Cataloging in Publication Data

Rauch, Gerry.
Handling Conflict.

1. Pastoral psychology. 2. International relations—Religious aspects—Christianity. 3. Conflict management—Religious aspects—Christianity. I. Title.
BV4012.R36 1985 248.4 85-14334
ISBN 0-89283-187-1

CONTENTS

Living as a Christian

IN HUMAN TERMS, it is not easy to decide to follow Jesus Christ and to live our lives as Christians. Jesus requires that we surrender our selves to him, relinquish our aspirations for our lives, and submit our will to God. Men and women have never been able to do this easily; if we could, we wouldn't need a savior.

Once we accept the invitation and decide to follow Jesus, a new set of obstacles and problems assert themselves. We find that we are often ignorant about what God wants of us as his sons and daughters. For example, what does it mean practically to obey the first commandment—to love God with our whole mind, heart, and strength? How can we know God's will? How do we love people we don't like? How does being a Christian affect what we do with our time and money? What does it mean "to turn the other cheek"? In these areas—and many others—it is not easy to understand exactly what God wants.

Even when we do know what God wants, it can

be quite difficult to apply his teaching to our daily lives. Questions abound. How do we find time to pray regularly? How do we repair a relationship with someone we have wronged or who has wronged us? How do we handle unruly emotional reactions? These are examples of perplexing questions about the application of Christian teaching to our daily lives.

Furthermore, we soon discover that Christians have enemies—the devil outside and the flesh within. Satan tempts us to sin; our inner urges welcome the temptation, and we find our will to resist steadily eroding.

Finally, we must overcome the world. We are trying to live in an environment that is hostile toward what Christians believe and how they live and friendly toward those who believe and do the opposite. The world in which we live works on our Christian resolve in many subtle ways. How much easier it is to think and act like those around us! How do we persevere?

There is a two-fold answer to these questions: To live successfully as Christians, we need both grace and wisdom. Both are freely available from the Lord to those who seek him.

As Christians we live by grace. The very life of God works in us as we try to understand God's teaching, apply it to our lives, and overcome the forces that would turn us aside from our chosen path. The grace we need is always there. The Lord is with us always, and the supply of his grace is inexhaustible.

Yet grace works with wisdom. Christians must *learn* a great deal about how to live according to God's will. We must study God's word in scripture, listen to Christian teaching, and reflect on our own experience and the experience of others. Many Christians today lack this kind of wisdom. This is the need which the *Living as a Christian* series is designed to meet.

The book you are reading is part of a series of books intended to help Christians apply the teaching of scripture to their lives. The authors of *Living as a Christian* books are pastoral leaders who have given this teaching in programs of Christian formation in various Christian communities. The teaching has stood the test of time. It has already helped many people grow as faithful servants of the Lord. We decided it was time to make this teaching available in book form.

All the *Living as a Christian* books seek to meet the following criteria:

Biblical. The teaching is rooted in scripture. The authors and editors maintain that scripture is the word of God, and that it ought to determine what Christians believe and how they live.

Practical. The purpose of the series is to offer down-to-earth advice about living as a Christian.

Relevant. The teaching is aimed at the needs we encounter in our daily lives—at home, in school, on the job, in our day-to-day relationships.

Brief and Readable. We have designed the series for busy people from a wide variety of backgrounds. Each of the authors presents profound Christian truths as simply and clearly as possible, and illustrates those truths by examples drawn from personal experience.

Integrated. The books in the series comprise a unified curriculum on Christian living. They do not present differing views, but rather they take a consistent approach.

The format of the series makes it suitable for both individual and group use. The books in *Living as a Christian* can be used in such group settings as Sunday school classes, adult education programs, prayer groups, classes for teen-agers, women's groups, and as a supplement to Bible study.

The editors dedicate the *Living as a Christian*

series to Christian men and women everywhere who have counted the cost and decided to follow Jesus Christ as his disciples.

BERT GHEZZI AND PETER WILLIAMSON
General Editors

ONE

We All Experience Conflict

Sunday, August 23, 1840. Have felt the past week several times as if I could no longer endure certain things that I find in my husband. . . . I suspect there is wrong on my part as well as his but I know no way to remedy it. . . . O that the Lord would show us the right way & incline our hearts to walk therein."

—the diary of Mary Richardson Walker*

MARY RICHARDSON WALKER and her husband Elkanah were missionaries to the Indians of Oregon during the 1830s and 1840s. Like Christians today, she and her husband struggled to build a strong relationship in the midst of difficulty and sin. Mary's diary leaves no doubt about the devotion and love with which she served her husband. On October 18, 1837, she

* *Women of the West*, ed. C. Luchetti (St. George, Utah: Antelope Island Press, 1982, pp. 70-71)

writes, "The thought of losing you has made me sensible how firmly the tendrills of my heart had become entwined, and how different from everything I before experienced is my regard for you" (p. 63), and on April 24, 1838: "May God help me to walk discretely, do right and please my husband" (p. 63).

Yet she did not know how to overcome the inevitable obstacles causing conflict in her marriage relationship. The editor of her diary notes that she and her husband "survived to form a loving and permanent relationship" (p. 61). It was a long, difficult struggle that could have been shortened if they had received the right Christian help.

Mary's good intentions were not enough; her love needed to be strengthened by wisdom. We are all in the same situation. Conflicts are sure to occur in our lives. Our intentions may be correct, our desire for unity and love may be beyond question, yet occasions of misunderstanding and hurt arise. Whether silly or serious, they are usually quite difficult to handle. We need to learn how to overcome them in a successful, Christian way.

Sometimes silly conflicts lead to major disruptions in our lives. In my first job after college one of my co-workers was also my best friend. When we were working together in public situations, I had the habit of dressing too casually. Whatever was most readily available on any given day I would wear, most often blue jeans and an old shirt. I was unconscious of the impact this might have on the people we were dealing with. One day my friend angrily told me how upset he was over the way I dressed. I could see he was right and started to dress in a more presentable way. But I also became afraid of his anger. I didn't know how to deal even with this small incident. Out of fear of his anger I started to drift apart from him. I didn't talk freely with him as I had in the past. As I became more guarded and self-protective, our friendship was withering away.

About two years later I began to learn more about Christ's teaching on personal relationships. In particular I learned that Christians should try to resolve conflicts in relationships directly. I was ashamed that I had let such a small incident produce such serious consequences. When I went to the other man and told him what had happened to me, it was very easy to restore our friendship.

More profound conflicts are more difficult to overcome. Yet Christians should not simply try to overlook them. Conflicts produce bad and broken relationships. Conflicts within the family threaten its stability and undermine the security and growth of family members. Conflicts in the work environment threaten careers. Conflicts in Christian groups destroy the ability of those groups to stay together and to serve God.

A recent year-end summary of a major news magazine used thirty-two photos to typify the preceding year. Twenty-four of those photos were directly related to stories of conflict—75 percent. But conflicts don't just occur in news-worthy world events. We all experience conflicts that have serious implications for our finances, our families, and our relationships.

If it were up to us, we might retreat from such conflicts. But it is no longer entirely up to us. Paul states the Lord's call this way: "Complete my joy by being of the same mind, having the same love, being in full accord and of one mind" (Phil 2:2). Shrinking back from conflict is ruled out. Rather, as Christians, we need to take up the task of "being in full accord and of one mind." We need to take up the task of making peace, and find the wisdom to carry it through.

We are not without hope for our relationships. Conflicts that threaten to separate us from friends or even family members need not have the last word. The Lord wants to teach us his ways so that we can become men and women of peace, effectively able to overcome conflict.

I remember the first time in my university years that I began to share an apartment with other Christians. We began with exuberance. Our commitment to Christianity meant the most to us of anything in our lives. Living with other students who had no great concern for their Christian lives left us dissatisfied. At last, we thought, here's the chance. When Christians live together, things should be so much better.

It didn't turn out exactly that way. There were more conflicts than before, more hardships. Why? It was harder because we were trying for something much deeper. Previously our relationships with our roommates had been on the periphery of our lives. Now we hoped for something much more together, and precisely in trying for it our own sins and failings came more to the forefront. We needed to learn how to handle the inevitable conflicts that arose between us in a way that was pleasing to God. This book summarizes what we learned.

Throughout the book I have included stories from my experience that will help the reader understand how the principles of handling conflict work in real life. But in deciding how to tell the stories I faced a certain problem. I could not be sure that everyone would want details of their lives told publicly. Most of the stories contained nothing that made me hesitate to include them, or I knew that the individuals involved would be glad to have their stories told. I was able to contact other individuals and get approval to include their stories. In a few cases neither option was open to me; I have told those stories with the names and circumstances changed. All the stories remain "true to life," and I think you will find they sound just like the things that happen to you and to those you know.

There are many approaches proposed today for conflict resolution. In this book we are going to attempt to follow the biblical approaches. We will look to the scriptures, both the New and the Old Testaments, for the Lord's teaching on how to deal with conflicts.

Therefore, this book is aimed at Christians. It may be useful in some ways to others also, but the teachings of the Lord inevitably call for conversion of life. The only way to reap the full benefits of his teachings is to sit at his feet in trust and faith. The Lord himself says, "My thoughts are not your thoughts, neither are your ways my ways, says the Lord. For as the heavens are higher than the earth, so are my ways higher than your ways and my thoughts than your thoughts" (Is 55:8-9).

Is the Lord's teaching, then, only useful for conflicts between Christians? Indeed there is a difference between handling conflicts with other Christians and conflicts with those who do not share the Christian point of view. But the Lord teaches us how to handle both situations. When we follow the Lord's teaching, we find that conflicts become opportunities for personal growth and often for improved relationships with others.

The opposite of conflict is peace, peace in our relationships with others. We need to begin by examining the scriptural notion of peace because it is often misunderstood.

TWO

Men and Women of Peace

ONCE A REPORTER was waiting to interview President Calvin Coolidge. The reporter obviously wanted to stir up something controversial that he could turn into a newsworthy story.

When the president finally appeared, the reporter asked, "Do you have any comments on your opponents in the presidential race?"

Coolidge answered, "No."

"Do you have any comments about the world situation?"

"No."

"Is there anything you can tell us about the battle over prohibition?"

"No."

Coolidge walked away but then stopped. He turned back to the reporter and said, "Now remember, don't quote me."

This is the same president who could say,

"Perhaps one of the most important accomplishments of my administration has been minding my own business."

I am not in a position to evaluate how much President Coolidge minded his own business. A president of the United States who minds his own business has a great deal of business to mind indeed, and a great deal of conflict to face. On the other hand, stirring up controversy where there need be none is not his business. But a reporter might look for a juicy tidbit of conflict from a president, because controversies and disputes make interesting stories. When the conflict is over, when the guns have stopped firing, when the slurs of a presidential campaign have ceased, when no banks have been robbed, then there is no front-page story.

Peace is usually in the news only for a short time. If two countries have been at war and a treaty is signed, then everyone rejoices that "peace" has been established. Yes, a certain kind of peace has been established. It is much better that no one is being killed any longer. But although armies are no longer fighting, the two countries may still hate each other just as bitterly. This notion of peace is not what the scriptures are speaking of when they mention peace.

Another inadequate notion of peace attempts to overlook wrongdoing for the sake of tranquillity. "Let's keep peace in the family" is often an appeal to an offended party to swallow an offence. No one is willing to try to resolve it. This is like sweeping dirt under the carpet: eventually the pile under the carpet is too big to overlook. Everyone can see that there's a funny-looking lump in the middle of the floor. The piling up of unresolved offences does not bring peace but separation and finally open hostility.

What is the biblical concept of peace? In the scriptures "peace" means more then simply the lack of open hostility or the overlooking of wrongdoing. "Peace" means a constructive, positive relationship that brings good for all involved.

As Christians we are concerned with peace because the Lord commands it. He wants us to seek peace with God and other men. Furthermore, the Lord gives us ways to make peace that non-Christians simply do not have. Peace, in turn, allows us to live fruitful lives.

We have all been shaped by the influences of the world around us. Now the Lord is calling us to an entirely different way of life. "Let the wicked man forsake his way, and the unrighteous man his thoughts. . . . For my thoughts are not your thoughts, neither are your ways my ways, says the Lord. For as the heavens are higher than the earth, so are my ways higher than your ways and my thoughts than your thoughts" (Is 55:7-9). He wants us to be shaped by his mind and by his ways.

As his sons and daughters, God wants us to be men and women of peace.

I once spent five years living with my family in another country. We had to learn many things in order to fit in, including a new set of manners. In America someone who invites guests to his house might put out drinks and snacks while everyone is sitting around talking. The guests know they are free to take the refreshments as they want. But in our new country waiting to be served in another person's home was a gesture of politeness. The host, in turn, showed honor for his guests by serving them. If you waited this way in an American home you would probably go hungry, and the host would wonder why you didn't like his refreshments. Needless to say we embarrassed ourselves quite a few times before we learned our new manners.

Differences in manners from one culture to another are not a matter of righteousness. We simply grow so accustomed to our own set of manners that we think they are the only natural ways to be polite. Immersed in the ways of our own native land we become blind to other ways.

In a similar way, we grow used to the ways of mankind and blind to the ways of God. As Christians we should want to follow God's ways. Differing with people of another culture over manners is not serious, but differing with God over how to live is serious. When our ways differ from his, we are in sin.

In matters concerning conflict and peace what are God's ways? Paul says, "I . . . beg you to lead a life worthy of the calling to which you have been called . . . eager to maintain the unity of the Spirit in the bond of peace. . . . Let all bitterness and wrath and anger and clamor and slander be put away from you, with all malice, and be kind to one another, tenderhearted, forgiving one another, as God in Christ forgave you. Therefore be imitators of God, as beloved children. And walk in love, as Christ loved us and gave himself up for us" (Eph 4:1, 3, 31-32; 5:1-2).

Notice that Paul asks us here to be "eager" to maintain unity in the bond of peace. It's not a question of a half-hearted desire that gives way before obstacles. When there's a difficulty or conflict, we need to be eager to see that it gets straightened out. We must value peace highly and pursue it actively.

What is an eager man like? What, for example, are the characteristics of a man who is eager for promotion in his career? He is diligent about his work and does more than is required. He looks for opportunities; he thinks about his career and plans for it. Therefore, he succeeds. That is the way we should pursue peace.

We should be eager for the peace the Lord

gives because it leads us to unity of spirit and oneness of heart. Peace binds us together in love. Furthermore, the Lord's way of life is able to bring peace. Under his authority every difficulty can be worked out. What a difference from our earthly expectations! Experience seems to teach us not to expect too much. Perhaps we've tried to resolve difficulties with others in the past and found that we only made things worse. We tend to think "it's best to leave well enough alone." But the Lord has a better way. He has good relationships in mind for us, and in him they can be achieved.

For example, consider how far we would go towards achieving peace if we followed the Lord's teaching through Paul in Ephesians 4:26. "Do not let the sun go down on your anger." He is saying if there is something wrong, see that it is straightened out before the day is over. Don't let it drag on. Unresolved problems that remain day after day lead to division and hostility.

The novel *Vipers' Tangle* by Francois Mauriac centers on unresolved problems between a man and his wife. The husband hears his wife calling out the name of another man while she sleeps. He thinks she feels burdened in their marriage and longs for the other man. Yet he never talks to her about the conflict within him. Instead of solving it before the sun goes down, he lives for years with the fear that his wife secretly despises him and loves another. The novel ends tragically with the conflict unresolved.

A married couple I know are very different. They consider it crucial to talk out difficulties as soon as they occur, even though their busy schedules interfere. Both the husband and the wife admit that it is often difficult to face their conflicts squarely. Yet they have done it.

The husband told me, "I know I am selfish and I often lack sympathy for my wife. I'm sure we would be tempted to separate if we hadn't tried to solve problems right away. A friend of mine who was getting divorced told me he wished he and his wife were as good as I and my wife are. But I know the difference between them and us isn't how good we are but that we don't let our anger build up against each other. I think the real difference is just that we handle the same personal problems they have in a different way."

In order to have peace the Lord also tells us, "Let all bitterness and wrath and anger and clamor and slander be put away from you, with all malice" (Eph 4:31).

Malice simply means hatred or hostility. Paul is saying we need to decide that malice will not be part of our relationships. Slander—speech against others—is also ruled out, along with strife, quarreling, and bad temper The world teaches us to accept these things as necessary evils. However, as Christians, we take our cues from the Lord, who tells us to put these things away for the sake of good relationships.

Note that I am saying that these things need to be ruled out of our relationships. That is, we need to rule out certain ways of *acting*. Some may think that the Lord is saying we need to tightly control our feelings. Yet the scripture does not say, "Thou shalt not have angry feelings." Rather, assuming we will experience anger, it says, "Don't let the sun go down on your anger."

While there is much to be said about feelings and emotions, that is not the topic of this book. Other excellent Christian books deal with those questions. (See especially *The Angry Christian*, by Bert Ghezzi, from Servant Books.) Rather, what I want to consider is how we can act in a way that resolves conflicts and establishes peace and good relationships.

Avoiding malice and strife does not mean giving up your strength. Rather it means using strength in ways that build up relationships instead of ways that tear them down. I have another close Christian friend whose early years were filled with strife. His older brother constantly bullied him; when he fought back, he lost. As a result, when he was older he would not give ground to anyone. He became a fighter, normally belligerent in his relationships with others, fighting about nearly everything. He wasn't channeling his God-given ability to fight to good ends.

When he became seriously committed to live a Christian life, he saw that he needed to change. He decided to stop constantly fighting. He still has a very strong personality, but now he uses his strength in a better way.

Most of us are not inclined to fight openly over everything as my friend was. However, we can easily fall into a pattern of quiet hostility. In most situations we avoid showing our anger but grow bitter when we are wronged. We need to realize that this "cold war" approach also damages relationships and separates us from other people. As Christians we need to avoid interior hostility as well as exterior hostility.

Two single women who live together, Mary and Sarah, told me about a conflict between them that their pastor helped them resolve. Mary went to her pastor to ask for help resolving a difficulty with Sarah. She began by telling him what she thought was wrong with her companion.

"I think Sarah needs to see a psychiatrist!"

"What's the problem?"

"She's obsessed with her flowers."

"Flowers?"

"It's probably not really the flowers. I think she doesn't know how to have good relationships so she puts all her time into flowers. She's obsessed with them!"

"What does she do?"

"She won't come in and greet guests if it's the last day she can get her tulips replanted. She made enemies with our neighbor whose Irish setter got into her flowers just once. She doesn't talk to me over breakfast. Instead she reads her flower catalogs."

"What does she say about it?"

"I haven't talked to her about it. I've always done everything I can to keep things good between us. So I've tried to do what she wants me to do. I even help her with her flowers. But I always have to do it just right or she's upset. Anyway I try to keep peace in our relationship. But all the accommodating has been on my side and I can't take it anymore."

Mary was trying to follow God's ways as she understood them. She thought of herself as someone who always tried to make peace. Yet her pastor could see she also needed to learn something else.

"Mary, I think you're overlooking something."

THREE

Speaking the Truth

In Ephesians 4:25 Paul states an important principle for resolving conflict: "Let everyone speak the truth with his neighbor, for we are members one of another." We might read this passage as simply forbidding lying, but there is more to it than that. It also directs us to do something, to speak. Lying is one way to violate this command, but withholding the truth is another. We should not keep important things from each other but speak openly.

Paul also gives a specific reason for this command. He says we should speak the truth because "we are members one of another." Christians are members of one another because they are together members of the body of Christ. There can't be real unity between the members of the body of Christ without knowing and understanding each other.

Dietrich Bonhoeffer said, "It is only when a man does not withhold the truth from another man that he is acting towards him like a brother. If I do not tell him the truth, then I am treating him as a heathen." There is a basic principle here: withholding the truth is a manifestation of division.

The biggest problem between the two women turned out to be that Mary was withholding something important from Sarah. Mary thought that in order to keep peace, she needed to hide her discontent. In turn, hiding her discontent led to misunderstanding.

"Here's what I think you should do," the pastor went on. "Sarah won't even know you're concerned about what she's doing unless you tell her. You've been trying to be accommodating so she probably thinks you're happy with everything. I would imagine a great deal of what looks obsessive to you has a good explanation, but an explanation you haven't heard because you haven't asked for it. You should talk to her about your concerns."

Of course everything can't be thoroughly discussed because there are limits to the time we have to communicate. Mary, however, had let matters of significance drift until she couldn't stand the situation. Sarah wasn't consciously offending her because she didn't know what Mary was thinking. Once Mary was willing to speak openly about her concerns with her, Sarah was genuinely interested and began to act differently.

I learned this same lesson in my own life. I once worked with a man who constantly criticized other people. I knew this habit was wrong but I never told him it bothered me. I tried to arrange things so that he and I never worked together. After about a year he realized something was wrong and asked me what was bothering me. When I told him, I was surprised to find out that he was aware of the problem and was trying to correct it. He wanted me to remind him not to criticize other people whenever I noticed it. By my lack of openness I had created a deepening rift between us and had withheld the help he wanted.

I am not saying that Christians are required to share all the intimate details of their lives with everyone, nor to pry into other people's lives. We should, however, communicate openly about whatever is significant in each of our relationships with those involved. Not everything is the business of everyone; different aspects of our lives will be appropriate to share in different relationships. But when it is appropriate, when we live together, work together, or serve together, then it is important for avoiding conflicts that we be open about our lives and our concerns.

A friend of mine named Scott once came to talk to me about a difficulty he was having. After joining our Christian group he learned that we encourage communication. He was having trouble with two members of the group and he knew he shouldn't keep problems inside.

"I'm having serious problems with Tom and Duane. I'd like to talk it over but I'd need to know that it would be kept between you and me."

"We really shouldn't do that," I responded.

"What do you mean? Aren't we supposed to be open with each other and help each other with our difficulties?" he asked.

"That's a different matter entirely. You're supposed to be open, and it's good to find someone who can help you with your own personal problems. But if you are having a difficulty with someone else, you should talk to the ones you're having a difficulty with. Maybe I could give you some advice about how to talk to them. But if you say it has to stay just between you and me, then that's not right."

"I don't understand why not."

"For one thing, it's not fair to them. If I hear your side of the story and I'm not allowed to hear theirs, then it gives me a bad image of them and they aren't able to defend themselves. I can't solve your problem with them either. You can solve it only with them."

"But I'm sure they wouldn't be open to what I have to say."

"Better at least give them a chance."

"I'd be afraid to do that."

"There are other things to be more afraid of."

"Like what?"

"If you don't talk to Tom and Duane, your relationship with them will stay tense, at least for you. And it will probably get worse. Anyway, it won't get better by talking just to me."

Scott didn't face up to this right away. Eventually he did, and when he talked to Tom and Duane they were able to take care of his concerns. Scott had misunderstood the direction to be open. He was willing to talk to me, but he wasn't willing, at first, to talk to Tom and Duane. It would have been easier for him to tell me his troubles and get my sympathy, but it would not have solved the problem.

One of today's popular approaches to problem solving recommends "getting it off our chest." Unburdening ourselves, even to strangers, is supposed to be therapeutic. Maybe we do feel better for a very brief time, but eventually we again have to face the people involved and the problem is still there. "Getting it off our chest" hasn't resolved anything.

When someone wants to "get it off his chest" to you, you are faced with another problem. He is drawing you into gossip. This is a hard situation to handle.

Sometimes I can easily find the right words to interrupt a situation of gossip but at other times it is more difficult. Often it's helpful to simply change the subject. One person I know constantly gossips. He isn't a Christian, and my relationship to him isn't close enough to permit me to confront him about his speech. To solve the problem I've learned to be ready with interesting topics to discuss whenever we are together. I can steer our conversations in a good direction because I'm prepared. Stopping his gossip would be more awkward if I weren't ready to set a better direction.

When gossip occurs in closer relationships, confronting it directly may be the best service we can render to the other person. There is much more to be said about proper and improper uses of speech than I have space to cover in this book. *Taming the Tongue* by Mark Kinzer (Servant Books) would be a very helpful book for anyone who wants to continue to explore the Lord's teaching in this area.

The scriptural direction for situations like Scott's is clear. The Lord gave us the principle himself: "If your brother sins against you, go and tell him his fault, between you and him alone. If he listens to you, you have gained your brother" (Mt 18:15). If Christians held themselves to following this teaching, less conflict would exist among Christians and a great deal more strength and peace would arise.

I've been involved in many cases where this

simple step has not only repaired relationships, but deepened and enriched them. I've seen reconciliation occur in difficulties over bad speech, over lost tempers, over incidents of drunkenness, over disputes about child-rearing, over lack of faithfulness on jobs, over irresponsibility in commitments, over borrowed and broken possessions, over disobedience to parents, and many other things. Following the Lord's teaching empowers us to overcome sin and stand united as Christians in our individual relationships, in our families, in our churches, and in our mission.

When we talk to someone about their wrongdoing, what do we do if they don't accept? First of all, we should listen to them carefully. They may see the situation in a way that is very different from our way of seeing it. Furthermore, we may be the ones who need to change.

In the first year of my marriage I had the habit of jumping to a lot of conclusions about what my wife did. Several incidents occurred in which I wrongly interpreted her behavior as disregarding my needs. I was later to find out that she was indeed thinking of my needs, trying very hard to care for me.

We were once returning from a long trip on which I was doing all the driving because she didn't yet have a license. I was tired and felt the need for a break. When I said I wanted to stop for a meal, my wife suggested driving farther before the break. I interpreted her response as insensitivity to my needs and got upset with her.

Later, when I was more open to hearing her side of the story, the situation looked very different. When we had set out that morning, I had made a big deal about wanting to get home quickly. She suggested that we drive farther before having a meal in order to do this. From her perspective she was helping me get what I wanted. She was concerned that we arrive early so that I would be pleased. I had been wrong to jump to the conclusion that she was being insensitive; just the opposite was true.

At other times the person we confront may simply not accept what they have done wrong. The Lord also gives us a direction for handling that situation: "But if he does not listen, take one or two others along with you, that every word may be confirmed by the evidence of two or three witnesses. If he refuses to listen to them, tell it to the church" (Mt 18:16-17).

Once again the procedure does not call for speaking against the other person. Rather, the Lord directs us to continue trying to settle the matter. This time we involve other witnesses. If that attempt also fails and the matter is serious enough, we can take the final step of bringing the issue to an appropriate authority for judgment.

A young woman named Beth told me about an

experience in which following the Lord's teaching kept her from losing a friend. She had volunteered two year's missionary service in her church in a poor area of the country where she worked with young people. Four women staff members were housed together, and their work went on successfully the first year. Two months into the second year Beth found that a hundred dollars was missing from her purse. She shared her room with another young woman named Lori and suspected Lori of taking the money, mainly because Lori seemed to have more spending money than usual just at that time.

Beth talked to Lori about the money, but Lori denied taking it. She claimed she was just spending money she had been saving for several months. The relationship of the two women became very tense. Beth had come to count on Lori as a close friend and didn't want the friendship to end this way. She also knew the Lord's teaching about seeking reconciliation and she determined to follow it.

Beth asked one of the other women on the staff to help in talking to Lori. The other woman had also noticed Lori had more money than usual and thought Beth was probably right about the theft. They went together to Lori, but again Lori denied that she had taken the hundred dollars.

Finally Beth went to talk to the pastor about the situation. He agreed to meet with Beth and

Lori. At last, with the pastor's help, a full picture of the situation became clear. Lori was indeed only spending money she had been saving. One of the girls who had attended a youth gathering at the staff house around the time the money was missing had a reputation for taking things. Neither Beth nor Lori had been aware of this girl's problem, but the pastor knew it and suspected the source of the difficulty right away. A phone call from the pastor to the girl's parents recovered seventy dollars still unspent, and the rest was restored later. Best of all, Beth and Lori's friendship was restored.

The teaching of the Lord is clear. When we have a charge against someone, we are to go to that person and seek reconciliation. In many cases we can avoid unnecessary divisions, as Beth did, by following the steps the Lord teaches us to take. Rather than leaving the problem unresolved, Beth continued to try to be reconciled with Lori.

Other conflicts may begin when someone has a charge against us. What do we do then?

In Matthew 5:23-24 the Lord says, "If you are offering your gift at the altar, and there remember that your brother has something against you, leave your gift there before the altar and go; first be reconciled to your brother, and then come and offer your gift."

Can it be that the Lord is saying that in all situations of conflict I am responsible for seeking out the other party involved? Yes, that's right. When we read both of these passages, we realize the Lord teaches that no matter who is at fault for the wrongdoing, I am responsible for seeking a reconciliation. As a Christian, the other person has the same responsibility if he is aware of the problem. But the fact that he has the same responsibility doesn't free me from my responsibility.

If a matter goes unsettled it's not enough to say, "Well, don't blame me. He didn't bring it up with me either." If I realized there was something to be settled and I didn't take action, I am at fault for the continuing break between me and that other person.

We all have the tendency to put the responsibility on others in every situation of conflict rather than take the responsibility on ourselves. Without realizing it we have contradictory attitudes in different situations.

When someone thinks we have wronged them we might say, "If he thinks I am wrong, why doesn't he come to me and tell me? I shouldn't have to go to him if he's the one who thinks there's something wrong."

On the other hand, when we think someone has wronged us we say the opposite. "He's the one who's wrong. Let him come to me to settle this. I didn't do anything so I shouldn't have to be the one to try to settle it."

The Lord teaches us that both of these attitudes are unrighteous. No matter who started the conflict or who is at fault, the Lord says we are responsible to go to the other party and seek reconciliation. In the rare instance when we need advice on how to resolve a conflict, we should seek the guidance of someone who can help us. We are not going for sympathy or to "get it off our chest" or to get someone on our side. We are going for help to know how to bring about reconciliation.

Even here we must be careful to avoid slander, which is speaking against another person. Under the guise of seeking advice we can be tempted to criticize the person with whom we have the conflict. We can avoid this temptation if our attitude is one of love, oriented towards restoring our relationship with the other person.

Finally, if we find ourselves needing this kind of advice regularly, it is likely that we have some other problem for which we should ask help. Are we allowing fear to keep us from going to a Christian brother or sister? Are we more interested in lowering the other person's reputation?

A young Christian man I know, named Jim, is very concerned to handle conflicts in the right way. He is conscientious in trying to speak only to the right people about problems and avoid slander and gossip. One day he called me on the phone sounding quite distraught.

"Do you have time for me to come over and see you?"

"Sure."

He was there in ten minutes, and he looked more bothered than I had ever seen him. As he unraveled his story about a work-related conflict I recalled that he worked in an office where almost everyone, including his boss, was a Christian.

"Everything was going fine at work till we got a new contract with First Federal Bank. All of a sudden Bill, my boss, is totally unreasonable about deadlines. Totally unreasonable. I can't meet them."

"Have you talked to him about it?"

"Yes, but he won't listen, and that's not like him. I'm under so much pressure that I can't even work well anymore. Then if I don't finish something on time he's really angry with me. I'm so tense about it. It's like a poison. I've tried to do the right thing. I haven't let the problem spread to anyone else."

"Is there anyone who can get involved and talk to Bill with you?"

"I tried that, too. He agreed that we could talk it over together with his boss, but his boss just agreed with him. I don't know what to do after that. I can't keep my bad attitude from becoming obvious to everyone at work. If it doesn't get straightened out, I know I'll start talking against him. I've tried to resolve this, but he just doesn't agree with me. I think he's really wrong to be treating me this way. A Christian should not be acting the way he is acting."

"Do you mean you think he's sinning against you in some way?"

"Yes. He's not treating me justly. It's not right to treat employees like this. I work as hard as anyone could, but I just can't do everything he's demanding. He's only concerned with the company's profits or something. So he's treating me unfairly and he won't listen. What can I do?"

"That's a good question."

FOUR

Resolving Matters of Right and Wrong

IT IS HELPFUL to understand that conflicts arise over all types of issues. Furthermore different types of issues need to be handled differently.

Sometimes a conflict involves objective right and wrong, based on God's laws. Since Jim's problem was work-related, let's take that area as an example. What is right and wrong in the area of work? What does the Lord teach us?

Paul wrote to the Thessalonians, "Now we command you, brethren, in the name of our Lord Jesus Christ, that you keep away from any brother who is living in idleness and not in accord with the tradition that you received from us. . . . We gave you this command: If anyone will not work, let him not eat. For we hear that some of you are living in idleness, mere busybodies, not doing any work. Now such persons we command . . . to do their work in quietness and to earn their own living" (2 Thes 3:6, 10-12). Refusing to work, or finding excuses not to be gainfully employed, are against God's law. This is a question of right and wrong, of sin and righteousness.

Other work-related matters do not involve objective right and wrong even if one course of action is clearly better than another. For example, it is almost always better to keep order in our work than to go at it haphazardly. Yet there is no law of God that makes it a matter of objective righteousness or unrighteousness. It is usually worse to approach work haphazardly but it is not a direct violation of any commandment of God.

Finally there are matters in which the best course of action is unclear and decisions are made simply according to personal preference. For example, while it's better to have order in our work than not to, which way of ordering our work we choose is simply a matter of preference.

Jim was unable to resolve his difficulty with Bill because Jim was seeing something as a matter of God's law that wasn't. Bill was a Christian, and Jim expected him to act in a Christian way. He felt sure Bill wasn't doing that. Jim had been unable to get through to Bill because Jim was insisting that Bill was sinning. Bill may have been acting unwisely, but he wasn't violating any commandment of the Lord.

"Jim, it doesn't seem to me like this is a matter of unrighteousness. Bill is the boss, and he can give direction to whoever works for him. But if your description is accurate, I would guess that he's making a certain kind of mistake."

"What is it?"

"It sounds to me like he's being unrealistic about how much you can do. He's within his rights to decide what to ask of you because he is in charge. It may not work out though. Your production will slump lower if he ruins your morale by demanding too much. It sounds to me like he ought to listen more to you about how much you can do in the time you have. But that's not a matter of unrighteousness. There's no law of God involved. His action might be ineffective, but it's probably not sinful."

Jim agreed that the conflict did not center around a sin of injustice as he had previously thought. His road was still tough for a short time. Bill was making an error, but it was easier for him to see the error when Jim stopped insisting it was sinful.

Conflicts occur in all three of the areas I have mentioned and have to be handled differently. In the following chapters we will consider how to handle conflicts about personal preferences and conflicts that arise over which approach is better than others. First, let's look more closely at conflicts in the area of sin and righteousness.

God's laws are the basis on which we can know what is objectively right and wrong. We need to know what his law is, because it has a priority that no other laws, directives, or reasonings have. God has revealed it as a way of life for us.

Jesus said, "Take my yoke upon you, and learn from me; for I am gentle and lowly in heart, and you will find rest for your souls. For my yoke is easy, and my burden is light" (Mt 11:29-30). A yoke ties an ox to the farmer's purposes. In a similar way God wants to yoke us to his purposes, his ways. But God's yoke is easy and light; being required to do things his way is a great good for us. All other ways, even if they seem better, turn out to be a burden that is not light or easy.

For example, following God's laws against gluttony and drunkenness is a great help. When we eat moderately our health is better, and we are more ready to do our work. When we avoid drinking immoderately we also avoid drunken bouts that destroy physical things or relationships. God's way of life is more enjoyable than eating and drinking to excess.

Our own pride and defensiveness often stands in the way of giving up our ways. Even when we know we are in the wrong, we can easily be tempted to hide it. Mary Richardson Walker's diary honestly expresses something each of us finds ourselves doing:

"January 20, 1838. Recd. a letter from my dear W. [She was still engaged to Elkanah Walker.] It contained such severe criticism as I almost feel as if I could not bear it. It is extremely mortifying for me to meet such reproof. . . . I will, therefore, bear it patiently and determine never to let any one have occasion to notice a repetition of the same. I will however retaliate a little by just letting him know that I have noticed a thing or two in him as well" (p. 63). Mary was embarrassed that Elkanah observed wrong in her life. But she did not just change the wrong, she also decided to get him back.

The Lord teaches us to resist this kind of tendency. "Why do you see the speck that is in your brother's eye, but do not notice the log that is in your own eye? Or how can you say to your brother, 'Let me take the speck out of your eye,' when there is the log in your own eye? You hypocrite, first take the log out of your own eye, and then you will see clearly to take the speck out of your brother's eye" (Mt 7:3-5).

There is a valuable lesson here for resolving conflicts over right and wrong. As a first step in any such conflicts, we should stop and search our thoughts to see if there couldn't be some wrong on our part. With a little effort at honesty we will usually find we are at least partially to blame. Then we should be quick to ask forgiveness. It makes a big difference in settling disputes when someone is willing to take the first step of admitting wrong. Unless we are absolutely convinced that we didn't do anything wrong, we should take the first step. By admitting even minor wrongdoing we can change the tone of a tense discussion. The other person is then more likely to be open to seeing his own wrongdoing and to feel free to ask for forgiveness also.

Most of us find it very hard to admit our wrongdoing when we first have to do it. However, after several times the difficulty diminishes a great deal. I know it was extremely difficult for me when I first openly admitted wrongdoing and sought forgiveness. Several years later a friend of mine was upset with me for delaying in giving him his part of the profits from some work we had done together. I knew he was right as soon as he pointed it out. I had had the money for about three months but had forgotten to send him a check. I immediately paid him, but I also asked him to forgive me. He was completely surprised because he thought I was going to defend myself and perhaps even try to cheat him out of the money. He forgave me, but then he said, "That must have been hard for you to admit you were wrong."

His remark made me think. It hadn't been hard at all. Looking back I realized that I had changed a great deal from my first uncomfortable efforts at owning up to wrongdoing.

(For more on the value of repentance in personal relationships see *How to Repair the*

Wrong You've Done, by Ken Wilson, from Servant Books.)

After we have admitted our own wrongdoing then we can address the wrongdoing of others with whom we might be in conflict. Point out what you think they are responsible for and ask them to correct it in whatever way is appropriate. While this is often as difficult as admitting and asking forgiveness for our own sins, it is the best way to resolve things. Say clearly and directly what you think is going on. Say it kindly and without animosity, but say it. The results are usually either that the other person has a good explanation you didn't know existed, or he is willing to admit what he has done wrong. Often these steps are all that is required to resolve a conflict.

On the other hand, sometimes they are not enough. If you can't resolve the matter with those involved, unless it is small enough that you should let it go, get a judgment from someone you both trust.

My wife and I once got angry with each other in front of our children. (When I say "once" I don't mean it was the only time this ever happened.) We managed to settle the difficulty and ask each other's forgiveness for our inappropriate anger. I also thought we should ask the children to forgive us for how we had acted. She didn't think that was necessary or helpful, but that the children should be able to see that we could have a problem between us and then resolve it.

We tried several times to discuss this question, but we could not see eye to eye on it. When a friend of ours whom we both respect came to visit us, we asked him for advice as a way of settling our difference. I expected that he would help me convince her of my point of view. I was surprised that he agreed with her. He pointed out that it was the two of us who had had the dispute and we had settled it. We didn't need to ask the children's forgiveness because they weren't the offended parties. They knew that it was settled between us, and that was enough.

In such situations, without the help of others our conflicts just persist. It is not always easy to know God's ways. We may feel absolutely sure we know what's right and wrong, yet be misinformed. Instead of letting a dispute drag on, it is good to turn for help to some third party who is more experienced than we are.

But not every difficulty between people involves matters that have a clear right and wrong. In those cases how do we resolve conflicts?

I had a college roommate, named Jack, who didn't like my habit of leaving clothes lying in a heap on my bed as I rushed out of our room to a game of basketball or touch football. I would come back to the room to find he had pitched them all into the middle of the floor. The message was clear. He disliked my leaving my clothes out of place. He wanted the room kept straight.

I was pretty defensive about it. There was nothing wrong with something being out of place for a while. The clothes were left on my bed, not on his. I had just as much right to have things the way I wanted as he had to have them the way he wanted.

We were two stubborn college freshmen, both sure we knew better. There was no clear right or wrong between our two approaches. How does one go about resolving such conflicts? I wish I had known then what I know now.

FIVE

Better and Worse

I SAW MYSELF as orderly enough, but Jack didn't agree. We had no way to settle the dispute. We compromised; I put away my clothes more often but not as much as Jack wanted. Neither one of us was very happy with the result. I was upset that he cared about it, and he was upset that I resisted what seemed obvious to him. The compromise avoided total division between us, but still our relationship was damaged.

I was stubborn about my point of view because there was nothing clearly wrong with what I was doing. If Jack couldn't demonstrate what was right and wrong, I felt completely justified in overlooking his concern. How should such a problem be resolved?

Looking back on it, I now realize that even though my behavior wasn't wrong—scripture doesn't teach any particular standards of neatness—I should have been open to improving the order of our room. Jack's approach was better than mine, and I would have done well to accept it.

Many conflicts occur over what's better and what's worse, even where no sin against God is involved. What does being on time mean? When should we arrive at a party and when should we leave? What are the proper ways to dress for different occasions? How soon does the car need to go in for a checkup? What are the priorities in home repairs? What do we need to spend our money on now? How should our office be arranged if we share it with someone else? What's too much noise? Do I keep my lawn nice enough for the neighborhood? Should the neighbor kids be allowed to walk over it? If we don't settle these kinds of questions, there can be just as much hostility between ourselves and others as there would be if sin were involved.

Pop psychology teaches that there are no objective standards, just personal preferences. If this is true, then all I need to do is follow my personal preferences. Education becomes "values clarification." We educate people by helping them clarify for themselves what values they prefer.

Such an approach reduces our human dignity by neglecting that we are able to make good judgments. Life is not just a chaotic stream of events. We can make good choices and decisions based on sound principles.

The trouble comes when people disagree about what is better and what is worse. When we are involved in disagreements over what is better, how do we resolve them? First of all, we should consider whether there is something we aren't doing well. If there is, we should be quick to acknowledge it. If we think others need to do better, we should tell them. Say it in a kind way, but say it directly and clearly so that they understand what you think.

Frequently a good discussion of the matter will lead us to a common conclusion with another person. Often the solution will be different than the original position of either person involved.

But there are many difficulties in which it is not clear what is the better solution. Several good approaches may be possible and none of them may be obviously better. In cases like this we can reach resolutions by making agreements. Consider this example from Mary Richardson Walker's diary:

> Tuesday, April 23, 1839. I feel vexed. This is the third morning I have omitted the sweeping when I first got up just to see if Mrs. E. [who was stationed at the same mission] would not take her turn. Sunday morning when I commenced sweeping she remarked she would have done it but supposed I had already. But the floor was so dirty had she looked at it she

> could not decently avoid sweeping. But some how she managed to get to the tubs & I would not be so impolite as to crowd her away, so while she was washing her clothes I just swept the room. This morning I wished to make haste & iron while babe slept so left an opportunity for her to sweep again. But I left it go till ten o'clock when she took her knitting & walked off after cracking & scattering about nut shells. So I have swept the room with a vengeance. I have washed the room every week while we have been here & she not once & I think she shirks more than is decent. Evening, have got plenty words to say. (p. 68)

Not knowing how useful it would be to make an agreement with Mrs. E., Mary became so frustrated with the situation that it seems she finally exploded in anger.

Agreements need to be made clearly. For example, if a group of people living together in an apartment agree in general that everyone will take responsibility to do the dishes, it probably won't work. Each one will have a different idea of what the agreement means. One thinks all are going to take turns. Another thinks whoever is home first will do them. Another thinks whoever has free time on an evening will do them. One person ends up doing them most often and feels resentful, or the dishes just don't get done.

Once an agreement is made we need to remind each other of it. The invariable rule is that people forget new agreements. Encouraging reminders strengthen the agreement until a new habit is formed.

I used to spend some time every day praying with a friend named Dave. We both liked a song that had the words, "Now the salvation, and the power, and the kingdom of our God, and the authority of his Christ have come." He invariably sang "has" for "have." It was an easy mistake to make. By the time you get through singing all those words you can forget that the subject is plural and so the verb should be plural. It's "salvation" and "power" and "kingdom" and "authority" together.

At first I thought I'd just put up with it. But day after day he'd sing it wrong. I should have been able to disregard it, but it bothered me. I wondered how a trivial thing like the wrong verb could disturb me so much.

One day before we started to sing I took the songbook and showed Dave that the verb was plural. That was fine with him, and we started our prayer time with the song. When we got to the verse in question, Dave sang "has" again as he had always done. Since we had just agreed to sing it the right way, I was sure he was rebelling against being told what to do.

I didn't pray very well that day. I thought he

had continued to sing the wrong verb on purpose, to resist me. When our prayer time was over I asked Dave why he had sung "has." It turned out that he had just forgotten. But he was glad to be reminded, and after that he always sang the song the right way.

Remember that new agreements usually aren't kept the first time. They take a bit of remembering and reminding. We shouldn't see that as a big deal. In most of the agreements I make with my wife I have to be reminded at least once before I remember to do what I have said I will do. It's not a matter of disregard for her so much as it is the force of habit. It takes some time before I get used to the new way of doing things.

Another type of difficulty that recurs with agreements is "the two expectations problem." An agreement seems to be clear enough, but the people involved have different expectations. A friend of mine told me how this had once happened on his job.

"I was working on a project with another man in which we shared the responsibility for the decisions and the work. We both reported to the same boss, but because his office was in another city, we were given pretty complete authority to run the project. We both thought our agreements about how to work together were clear.

"We were discussing a decision one day, and

my co-worker proposed something I just could not accept. He said he was going to do it anyway because it needed to be done. I was shocked that he would say that. I thought we were supposed to agree on decisions before acting, and I told him so. He said he thought he had a right to make a decision if the two of us didn't agree. We had a good relationship with each other and still do, but neither one of us would budge. We had both heard the same briefing from the same boss, but we came away from it with two ideas of what would happen in the event of a disagreement.

"I then yielded to his decision, but I wanted the approach to be cleared up with our boss. We had to wait till he was in town. When we did get to talk to our boss, he confirmed that the other man was supposed to decide what to do if we weren't in agreement. How did I miss that? I don't know, but I did."

Making agreements, making them clearly, and reminding each other of them can go a long way towards resolving conflicts when there is no objective standard to indicate what is the best decision.

One prominent woman, Sally Ride, seems to have been partially influenced in her career direction by a shock to her expectations when she took her first babysitting job. *Newsweek* reported that "the first time S. baby-sat, her father recalls, her charges refused to eat the sandwiches she prepared because she put the peanut butter and the jelly on in the wrong order. She threw the sandwiches out, made another batch, and never baby-sat again."

SIX

Preferences

IN JUNE 1983 Sally Ride became America's first woman in space. But what was going on with those peanut butter sandwiches? Is it better to put on the peanut butter or the jelly first? Why did it matter to the children? Of course neither order is better or worse. It mattered to the children simply because of childish preference. But it was a preference that caused enough hassle to end Sally Ride's baby-sitting career.

Life includes such a wide variety of preferences, and preferences are often so inconsistent that God may have given them to us as opportunities to grow in holiness. Conflicts over preferences may not be the biggest conflicts we encounter, but they are probably the most common. They are the constant light skirmishes in which we practice conflict resolution so we will be ready for the full-scale battles over righteousness.

Probably most husbands and wives feel they were simply created different from each other.

My wife and I do. She likes to take walks in the sunshine; I like to walk in the shade. She likes the room as cool as possible at night; I like it "comfortably warm" (as I would call it). She loves liver; I can't stand it. She likes to drive if she's dropping me off; I prefer to drive till I get out and then turn the car over to her. She squeezes the toothpaste tube and I roll it. The list could go on and on.

How does one handle these kinds of differences? In general we should resolve such differences by giving way to others' preferences. In relationships where both parties are giving way the result is like Paul's teaching, "Outdo one another in showing honor" (Rom 12:10).

One of my friends, Dick, used to live in a house where he shared part of his driveway with a neighbor. Beyond the shared part of the driveway, two separate parts led to their respective garages. The neighbor didn't want anyone who came to Dick's house to stop in the shared part of the driveway, even for a short time. Even if someone was coming just to drop something off, that was too long. Dick gave way to his neighbor's desires. He always told his friends to park back by his garage or in the street. Dick never became close to his neighbor, but his willingness to give way made a big contribution toward peace in their relationship.

It helps to have a sense of humor about

preferences. The more we are attached to our preferences, the sillier we are. That seems obvious when we consider the preferences of others but not so obvious when our own preferences are at stake.

The children who didn't want Sally Ride's peanut butter sandwiches were acting childishly, but not so much because they had a preference. How different is the preference for putting on the peanut butter first and the jelly second from my own preference to walk in the shade instead of in the sunlight? Rather those children were acting childishly because they were so attached to their preference that they wouldn't eat the first batch of sandwiches. One sign of maturity is the ability to overlook our own preferences when that is necessary.

If we think someone else is inordinately attached to their preferences, we would do well to consider whether we are not the ones who are too attached to our own preferences.

I was once on a trip with two friends. We had taken one road map along with us. On the way, while one of them was driving the other one was looking at the map. I told him I wanted to see it when he was finished, but he went on looking at it for some time. I began to get upset. I started to think he wasn't being considerate of me and that he was too attached to looking at the map. But then something hit me. Why was I so upset?

Because I was too attached to seeing the map myself and I wasn't being considerate of him.

In a dispute over preferences it's hard to tell who's being too attached to their own way. Frequently it's both sides who are too attached. Either party can easily say, "You're making too big a deal of this." If we ever find ourselves saying something like that, then probably we ourselves are guilty of making it too big a deal. How can we accuse the other party of being unwilling to give up their preference when we aren't willing to give up ours?

When we are under someone else's direction, for example at work, it is especially good to give way. Once a man I worked for asked me to find out his flight schedule, and I agreed to do it. I went on with the bit of writing I was finishing. I noticed that after about five minutes, he called the airline himself and found out what his schedule would be. I realized then that when he asked for something, he preferred to have it done right away. After that I made sure to do it his way.

Oftentimes we can find a workable compromise when our preferences clash. One of my college roommates liked to go to sleep with the stereo playing. He would put on a stack of records and be asleep before the first one was over. I couldn't sleep with the music playing, but I knew it was the way he wanted to go to sleep. I resolved the problem by waiting till I could tell he was asleep and reaching over to reject the rest of the records. Soon I would be asleep, too.

Sometimes conflicting preferences result from different points of view. My wife and I try to do something together with our children on Saturday afternoons. She always preferred to do something away from our house. On the other hand, I preferred to do something at home. Our preferences were different because she was at home most of the week caring for the children and I was away because of my work.

I yielded to her preference, and after some time my own preference changed. On Saturday afternoons we had had some wonderful experiences and had visited a lot of interesting places. Each excursion was a delightful memory. I found out that yielding to her preference led to a change in me. I liked the new way of doing things better than the one I would have chosen previously.

Another area that can lead to disputes is personality differences. I once had occasion to travel to Africa as an assistant to a Christian leader who was going there to meet with several individuals and groups.

After a stunningly beautiful flight over the Sahara we landed in Ghana. It was the hottest season of the year. In the airport it was impossible for us to detect what principles of organization guided the flow of people and luggage. Everything looked like a big melee. Others were making progress through it, but we had no sense of what to do.

The person we were to visit, a European living in Ghana, found us in the crowd. He was able to help us make some progress but still painfully slow. Finally, a Ghanaian appeared to help us, a friend of a friend of our European host. Somehow he knew we would be there, although none of us had requested him to come. Since he knew the right way to get through everything, we were soon standing at the door of the airport with luggage in hand and our "angel" disappeared into the crowd. We never saw him again.

By this time I was tired, and the heat was getting worse. We got into a van with our host and began a long drive to another city. I was exhausted and wanted to put my head down to sleep. The man I was with, however, was just starting to come alive. I couldn't believe it. After a long airline flight, the airport ordeal, and the heat, not to mention the confusion of a totally new atmosphere, he was energetic, enthusiastic, and talkative.

I began to wonder if it was a mistake that I had come along on this trip. If I had to do it the way he was doing it, I thought I would collapse. This was the first day of a month-long trip, and already I felt exhausted. His enthusiasm made me feel even more exhausted. The brighter and cheerier he got, the more depressed and hopeless I felt, because I just couldn't do what he was doing.

I would have preferred to be lively like him. I admired his energy and his interest in the people we were meeting. During the rest of the trip I always felt guilty for how that first day had gone. There were also some others like it. I thought I should have been able to be like my travel companion.

It was only later that I realized what had been going on and how to understand it. It wasn't something I should have felt guilty about. It was simply a difference in personalities. The personality differences between me and the man I was assisting were the reason for the differences in our responses to what we encountered. Neither response was right or wrong, better or worse.

People's personalities are different. Even identical twins have different personalities from each other. Some personalities are a lot like some others, yet many are vastly different. Some personalities get along with each other, and some clash with each other.

Even though personality differences can sometimes result in conflicts, they can also enrich our lives. By themselves, differences in personality don't cause conflicts. Rather our bad responses to personality differences cause conflicts. We should learn the right way to respond to these differences and gain the riches they can provide.

The human body presents an analogy of differing personalities. Each muscle has a corresponding muscle in tension with it, ready to pull the opposite way. To coordinate the body, one muscle has to relax while the opposite muscle tenses. This is not a problem for the body, but is the very reason why it can function.

Our relationships with others who have different gifts and personalities is similar. The many contributions each person makes can enrich our life together just because of the differences. If we are limited to our own insights and ways of acting, then society would not function well. But we need wisdom to know when to exert our own personalities and when to relax and be quiet, letting others exert their personalities.

My children, too, were born with different personalities. I could see differences from the first days after each was born. No doubt they will grow up to be similar in many significant ways. Nonetheless my wife and I won't always treat each of them exactly the same way, no matter how hard we might try. Each of them will also face different life circumstances and make different choices. God's grace will work differently in each of them. No matter how much they are like each other, they will also be different.

I once worked with another man named Tony whose personality was very different from mine. Sometimes the differences seemed too great a problem to both of us. As he put it, no matter what he proposed to do he could count on me to question it from an entirely different perspective. I felt the same way.

After working together for a couple of years, however, we realized our differing perspectives were a source of richness and safety. Each of us could do things the other couldn't. If we could agree on something, it was probably a very good idea. Neither of us would have wanted to be without the different contributions the other one made.

How do people with differing personalities stay together? They stay together by being committed to working for the unity God wants them to have, by having the wisdom necessary to work out the problems that come up, and by being open to the work of the Holy Spirit. A relationship that fails because of personality differences probably lacks strength in one of these areas.

Sometimes we may accept negative comments we hear about someone else whose personality is quite different from ours. We should guard ourselves against this. I once heard some negative accusations about a friend of mine that I should not have heard. I tried to forget the accusations, but I couldn't. Slowly I was turning against him. Because I didn't like what was happening and knew it was wrong, I prayed and asked God to help me. Soon I started to see this man in a new light. I actually started to have a great deal of respect for him. I saw how strong certain areas of his life were, and I began to learn a lot from how he did things.

After my attitude about him improved, I asked myself why I had been so affected by the negative things I had heard about him. I realized I had been open to taking what I heard in a negative way simply because he did things so differently from me.

In chapter four we considered conflicts that arise over matters of right and wrong according to God's law. In chapter five we looked at conflicts over better and worse ways of doing things. In this chapter we have discussed conflicts that arise because of differences in preferences and personalities. I want to make clear that the resolution of all different types of conflict depend on what the conflicts are about. We handle different types of conflict differently because the nature of the disputed material is so different.

But not all conflicts can be resolved in these ways. A married couple who I know once got into a complicated difficulty. They had been neighbors and close friends for years with an elderly widow whom they dearly loved. She had even been like another grandmother to their children.

As she grew older she had become less and less flexible about how she wanted things done. Her ways and their ways began to impinge on each other. One day an incident occurred that threatened the couple's relationship with the elderly widow. She normally worked in her yard for a few hours early in the morning. They were setting out for a day's excursion with their family but wanted to water the side of their yard toward her house. They asked if she would turn off the water at the end of her time working. She gladly agreed to do it.

But she didn't turn off the water. It ran all day. They arrived back home about midnight and went straight to bed without noticing that the water was still on. It ran all night. Because the land between the two houses sloped her way, some of the water got into her basement.

The next day she was furious with them. She demanded that they apologize, come and clean up, and buy her a new couch to replace one she claimed was ruined by the water. They cleaned up her basement but couldn't see that any damage had been done. The water didn't seem to have reached as far as the couch. It looked to them like the couch had only deteriorated because of being in her damp basement so long. When they reminded her that she had promised to turn off the water, she denied it.

This looks like a lot more than a personality

conflict. Her personality was changing with advancing age, but the incident reflected more than a personality conflict.

My friends solved their problem, though. What would you have done?

SEVEN

Forbearance

MY FRIENDS DECIDED it would be best to simply put up with how their neighbor was acting. They decided to forbear and not try to correct her. Their decision is a striking example of the right kind of Christian forbearance.

Their elderly neighbor was indeed being unreasonable. With advancing age, she was changing, forgetting things that were essential and important to others while rigidly maintaining she was in the right. My friends started to look for a couch for her at garage sales and found a nice one at a low price. They bought it, and she was very happy with it. They also decided not to rely on her in the same way as before.

What surprised me at the time was how happy they were to do all this. They fully accepted going the extra mile for her. It was a source of joy to them to be able to be kind to her. When we forbear from the heart, it does not cause us to feel burdened or resentful.

Forbearance is an important Christian response to many of the difficulties we face. There are times when it is right for us to put up with difficulties even if some wrong is involved. It would be impossible to correct everything that causes us problems.

In Colossians 3:12-13 Paul says, "Put on then, as God's chosen ones, holy and beloved, compassion, kindness, lowliness, meekness, and patience, forbearing one another and, if one has a complaint against another, forgiving each other; as the Lord has forgiven you, so you also must forgive."

The Lord is the model for us. As he had a heart to forgive us even before we asked for forgiveness, we should have a heart to forgive others even before they ask us. We should forbear the many faults and weaknesses in all those with whom we have contact. We should forbear especially when we have difficulties with others' preferences, mannerisms, or smaller failings. Whenever we are close with other people, we will encounter preferences and mannerisms different from our own. Other people will have the same kind of problems with us.

Situations in which we have to forbear are like God's sandpaper in our lives. Just as sandpaper takes off rough edges, making the effort to put up with others takes off the rough edges of our character until our imperfections are removed. All of us are set on having some things just our way, consciously or unconsciously. Part of what the Lord is doing is breaking us of that kind of willfulness.

When I speak about breaking, I do not mean "breaking down" or "crushing in spirit." Rather the image I have in mind is like the breaking of a wild horse. The trainer doesn't try to demolish a horse's spirit, but he tries to tame it so that it can be used. In our relationship with God we need to be brought to the point where our personal preferences and idiosyncracies do not get in the way of God's plan for us. After he applies the "sandpaper" to us, we are able to do a lot more for him. We're able to relate in a more selfless way. We're able to be flexible and adapt to other people's needs instead of putting our preferences first.

Something else that helps us handle small problems is putting them in perspective. Not everything that bothers us is really all that important. If you are distraught about something small it may help to compare it to something more serious. For example, you might ask yourself, "Why am I more upset about my husband being five minutes late than I am about the drug problem in our country?" The extra five minutes you have to wait appears as the small thing it really is when it is put next to something profoundly important.

When we should forbear because the matter is

not significant enough to be dealt with, it may be helpful to recall how the Lord treated us with forbearance. He put up with our sinful condition so that he could redeem us. If he hadn't been willing to do that, we would still be in the condition of "having no hope and without God in the world" (Eph 2:12). If we are going to forbear in small or large trials, we need to do it willingly. It's easy to miss this point and develop a "martyr complex" instead. Feeling sorry for ourselves, or allowing resentment to take over, we might think, "It's *so* hard to bear with all of John's idiosyncracies. I've had to put up with so much. I hope someday he has to face up to what he's doing." But that isn't forbearance. Genuine forbearance is done willingly. When we forbear, we decide that it is not best to try to deal with the problem and that the matter isn't important enough to upset our relationship with the other person. We need to put any wrong done to us out of our mind in a way that really puts the matter to rest. It is over. We hold no grudges about it that might surface later on.

That is what forbearance entails. We are not forbearing if we remain angry with the other person involved. To remain angry is resentment. If we cannot forbear in the sense that the matter is really put to rest, then perhaps we should not be trying to forbear. It may be that we should speak to the other person and try to resolve the difficulty. While the Lord teaches us that there are many cases in which we should forbear, there is no value in fooling ourselves. If we are unwilling to address a problem, it doesn't help to call our unwillingness forbearance. If the problem is not really put to rest, it will probably surface again.

In a case like this it is usually better to handle the problem by directly discussing it with the other person involved than by trying to continue to forbear. Our inability to forbear may be a sign that we should not be trying to forbear.

Once I was working in a situation where I had to supervise eight people. There's an old proverb that says, "the squeaky wheel gets the oil." Among those eight people I had a lot of "squeaky wheel" situations to care for. My time and attention were thoroughly taken up with managing just the urgent matters that arose each day. As a result there were at least two of the eight people who didn't get much help from me for their work.

One of the ones who I didn't give much help to was Peter, who happened to be a Christian. He could see how I was constantly buried with urgent matters, but after several months he was having a harder and harder time being satisfied with the situation. He felt that he should be able to accept that I was not giving him the help he needed because of the other needs. But he found it bothering him more and more.

He finally asked to talk to me and in a respectful way told me that he wanted to be able to accept the situation as it was but was having a very hard time doing it. In some way he thought it was wrong of me to neglect directing him even though there seemed to be good reasons for what I was doing.

It was good that Peter talked to me because, without seeing it, I had been caught in something that someone has called "the tyranny of the urgent." I had let a lot of important matters slip because of the "tyrannical" way that matters of lesser importance demanded immediate attention. Rather than just oiling every wheel that squeaked, I should also have been taking care of various matters of more importance that weren't constantly clamoring for attention. For one thing I should not have left Peter unsupervised for several months.

Peter had been trying to forbear in the situation. When he felt that he couldn't continue forbearing, it was a good sign that forbearance wasn't called for in this case. It was better to bring the difficulty to my attention.

The goal of forbearance is not that we should give way to sin but that we should be able to distinguish between matters of greater and lesser significance and know when to attend to each. There is a lot of room to forbear with others in all the little trials of life. This does not change what I have said earlier in the book about having the courage to speak directly to others about difficulties when there is some matter of significance involved.

Sometimes people overdo avoiding difficulties in the name of forbearance. Tom and Kevin were two men I knew who went into business together. Things seemed to go very well for the first year, but then Tom came to me for advice on how to work out a difficulty he was having.

"I don't think our financial arrangement turns out to be fair for me. I did agree to it, and I knew at the time that it wasn't quite evenly balanced, but just to make things go well I agreed to it. It's mostly been going fine, but now Kevin wants to make some changes on his part that will drastically hurt me. If I hadn't agreed to the uneven split this would not have come up. I didn't realize he would ever want to make changes. I guess he's within his rights to make changes, but if he does, it will be a disaster for me."

"But you agreed to it in the beginning?"

"Yes, there was a reason for that. We were both convinced we should go into this business, and it has turned out to be good. It's a success. But we had a very hard time figuring out a fair break on the finances. Also the timing of starting the business was important, so I proposed this arrangement just so he would accept it and we could get started. I didn't think there was any other way to break the logjam. I was willing to accept a slight imbalance.

"Now every day since he has started to work on this change I'm really upset. He doesn't know it, but I'm resentful whenever I see him."

At first I started to think of how Jesus had refused to get involved when he was asked to help settle the division of an inheritance. Tom and Kevin's difficulty sounded complex, and I would have preferred not to get involved. I would have been very glad to say it was none of my business. But then I recalled some incidents from Tom's past. I had known him very well for about eight years, and now, all of a sudden, I could see a pattern in some of his behavior. I realized he frequently tried to forbear when it wasn't the right choice.

"Tom, do you realize this is just like some things you've done before?"

"No."

"I remember something about your previous job. You told me that for the last year you accepted a salary which was too low because you realized finances were tight in your department. You were never happy about it. Also I remember when you cut down a tree in your yard. You liked the tree but your neighbor put pressure on you to let his garden get more sunlight. You never really agreed it was necessary."

"What are you trying to say?"

"I think you should thank God for this problem in your business because I'm sure he's going to use it for your good."

"Thank God for it? You had better explain what you mean because I don't get it."

EIGHT

Thank God for Difficulties

IN THE MIDST of relationship difficulties we need to open our hearts to the other people involved, but we also need to exercise wisdom. Scripture says the Lord wants to give us wisdom. "If any of you lacks wisdom, let him ask God, who gives to all men generously and without reproaching, and it will be given him" (Jas 1:5).

No personal relationship difficulty has to be a defeat for Christians. Even the ones that are the most difficult often bring the greatest good if we approach them in the right way. I could see that this was the case for Tom, even though he thought there was little hope for the situation.

Tom had a certain way of acting that seemed good to him, even holy and righteous, but it didn't come from the Lord. The problem with Kevin was an opportunity for him to understand where he was missing the mark and an opportunity to change.

I went on, "Tom, I think you'll get more out of this if you are thankful for it."

"I'll try."

"What I just realized is that you're attempting to make peace in the wrong way. You agree outwardly to things that you don't really agree to inwardly. You seem to think you should always be the first one to give way to bring about peace. But it doesn't turn out to be a true peace because the things you agree to aren't what you really think. In a way it's not fair to the other people involved. If you say yes to something, they naturally take it to mean you agree. There's no reason for them to think otherwise. I'm sure Kevin never wanted you to get an unfair deal in your financial arrangements."

"Why do you say it's like those other situations?"

"You didn't think your salary was fair on your last job, but you still agreed to a lower one. You didn't think your neighbor's garden was in a place where it would be affected by the shade from your tree, but you cut down the tree anyway. I'm sure your former boss doesn't realize you think you were unfairly treated. All he knows is that you agreed to the salary. Your neighbor thinks it was just fine for you to cut down your tree."

"You're right."

"Kevin doesn't want you to be treated unjustly. I'm sure he wants to have a fair arrangement with you. But in any case, you should thank the Lord for bringing this out.

"I think you should go back to Kevin and tell him everything from the start. This time don't keep anything back. If you can work it out with him, you can learn how to do it in other situations. You should especially thank God that you get to work out the situation with Kevin. I'm sure he'll be a lot more open to it than someone who's not a close Christian brother."

Kevin was willing to renegotiate their financial relationship in a fair way. Tom is still learning to stick up for what he really thinks when he's making agreements, but the incident with Kevin got him started in the right direction.

In Romans 8:28, Paul says, "We know that in everything God works for good with those who love him." Commenting on this passage, Augustine says that even our sin can result in some good if we love God; that is, those who repent of their sin and turn back to God find that God uses the problems their sin has created for good.

Even before we repent, the problems arising out of our sins can be a discipline that helps us become open to change and repentance. There's no difficulty, whether it comes from our own sin or the sin of others, for which we can't genuinely thank the Lord in faith. He can use all things for the good.

Christians tend to think that any difficulty in personal relationships is a serious defeat. We regard any conflict, even the smallest one, as a great tragedy. We may begin to think that our Christian life is not worth anything because we lost our temper or because someone is not on speaking terms with us for a short time.

There are two paths to choose from when a conflict comes up. We may become alarmed and discouraged, but that is neither a response of faith nor helpful to resolving the conflict. Or we can choose the path of faith, recognizing the conflict is something to take seriously yet believing that God can work through it. We can expect in faith to see the fruit he will bring out of this difficulty.

These are two very different attitudes.

Through our difficulties the Lord wants to make us men and women of peace, patience, meekness, and humility. When necessary, he wants us to be able to deal with difficulties directly. He also wants us to be able to put up with difficulties when a situation calls for forbearance. He wants us to have an inner freedom so that the pressure of a situation doesn't dictate our actions. We don't just return anger for anger, hurt for hurt. He wants us to be free to discern what is the best way of acting and then respond in that way.

This takes an inner strength of Christian

character. It is not always easy to handle conflicts in the way the Lord himself would handle them. It is more common for human beings to be driven by their own preferences, habits of sin or idiosyncracies.

Take a new perspective on difficulties. If you approach them in faith, the Lord will use them for good, to build more loving relationships and to make you the kind of person he wants you to be.

The people in the Christian group I am part of were excited as we first began to learn how to resolve conflicts in our relationships. We found a new ability to relate well to one another. Just a few years previously we had continually run into obstacles that seemed insurmountable. Unresolved differences between us had threatened to drive us apart. As we learned how to overcome conflicts we found that our group became stronger. We were enthusiastic about what we were learning.

Some of us tried to start using the same approaches with our families, on our jobs, in our neighborhoods, or with our friends. It didn't work. At least we found out it didn't work the same way. How should we adjust our approach when we have difficulties with people who are not aware of how the Lord teaches Christians to resolve conflicts?

I once moved into a new neighborhood with

my family. At first we didn't know anyone who lived there. We decided to invite our neighbors to a party so we could meet them. One of the men who came to that party was a fireman. He had a good time at the party but it wasn't long before our relationship with him went sour.

One day, in our first winter in the neighborhood, I had not shoveled the snow off my sidewalk. Several inches had fallen the night before. This man never walked by my house, but he noticed the walk was not shoveled.

I heard through a third party that my neighbor was very angry with me. He had lost his temper, not directly at me, but about me, in front of the one who reported it. He was right about the sidewalk, of course. I should have shoveled it. There was even a city ordinance that required everyone to shovel their walks for the safety of anyone who might walk by.

After I heard he was angry, I decided to clear off my sidewalks diligently from then on. I made a few attempts to talk with him and repair our relationship. But he wouldn't give me any opening to directly address his complaint. I was sure he noticed that I was now shoveling my walk. I thought that would make him happy. Yet somehow he wasn't, and our relationship wasn't cleared up.

Christmas came. In the past I had usually gone caroling with my family in the neighborhoods where we lived. We decided to do the same in our new neighborhood. We set out and were having a great time. What would happen at the fireman's house? We rang the bell and started to sing as we had everywhere else. He and his wife came to the door, but when he saw who it was, he disappeared and wouldn't listen to us sing!

Now I felt worse than ever about the difficulty between us. He hadn't let me talk to him about the problem, although it was obviously important to him. The relationship stayed that way until spring when a simple solution presented itself.

NINE

Conflict Involving Non-Christians

RESOLVING CONFLICTS works differently when the conflict is with someone who does not share your Christian views. Although the other person involved may be a Christian, if he has not had any experience in dealing with conflicts in a Christian way, he may well misunderstand what you try to do.

I realized that since my neighbor did not consider himself to be a Christian at all, he was not interested in handling conflicts directly as I had been learning to do with other Christians. One day as I was out for a walk with my children, we happened to pass his fire station. He had mentioned at the party at my house, in fact, that he was the one in charge of that station. I knew the children would be excited to see how a fire station worked. It occurred to me that this might be an opportunity to soften the relationship with him.

I walked in with my two children and went to his office. I greeted my neighbor warmly and asked if there was any possibility the children could see the fire station. As I had hoped, he was delighted. Enthusiastically he took them to see everything in the fire station. I'm sure they got a better tour than would usually be given. The children loved every minute of it, and he seemed more delighted the further we went. From that day on our relationship was restored. He didn't want to talk directly about the snow shoveling incident, but he did want our relationship to be restored.

Why hadn't he been willing to talk about the matter directly? Without some help and encouragement people usually don't address their difficulties with others directly. In most cases it probably comes from bad experiences in previous conflicts. Most people haven't received any instruction about how to handle difficulties with others. For example, in situations of conflict most people would not admit their own wrongdoing first. Furthermore, they don't expect others to be open to seeing their own wrongdoing. If they tried to discuss a difficulty, they would probably expect the other person to be defensive and angry, rationalizing away any wrongdoing on his part.

My neighbor probably would not have expected me to admit I had been wrong in not shoveling my sidewalk. It is more likely that he would expect me to come to him in angry confrontation if I came at all. He might have expected me to say something like the following:

"I want to talk to you about this snow shoveling business. I was busy the other day so it took me longer than usual to get to it. You didn't have to get angry about it. And I don't know why you didn't come and talk to me about it first instead of blowing off steam to someone else."

Is he likely to have expected what I would have said?

"I wanted to let you know that I agree with you; I should have shoveled my walk. I'm sorry it was a bother to you. I want to make sure you know that from now on I'm planning to shovel any new snow as soon as I'm home to do it."

Why did going to the fire station help the relationship when Christmas caroling had failed? It may sound paradoxical, but in conflicts it is often easier for people to offer kindness rather than receive it. They are more sure of themselves if they sense that they have something to give. Receiving our kindness at Christmas was harder for my neighbor than being kind to us. The opportunity to give a tour to my children enabled him to relax and restore our relationship.

I don't present this story as an example of the ideal way to resolve conflicts. Rather I am trying to show that not everyone is ready to accept a direct approach. When we are handling difficulties with people who don't approach them the same way we would, the Lord still wants us to relate well to them. We have important interactions with co-workers, friends, neighbors, roommates, family members, and others. Many of these people will not want to handle difficulties directly. In these cases it is still vital that we do all we can to maintain good relationships.

Resolving conflicts with Christians who have been trained to do it the Lord's way is different from trying to resolve conflicts with those who approach conflicts in a different way. In scripture we find passages that address both situations. First Peter 1:22 says, "Having purified your souls by your obedience to the truth for a sincere love of the brethren, love one another earnestly from the heart." Here the concern is with "love of the brethren." "Brethren" is the New Testament word for fellow Christians. It is sometimes used in scripture to speak of blood family members, but most often it is used to speak of Christians.

On the other hand, Colossians 4:5-6 says, "Conduct yourselves wisely toward outsiders, making the most of the time. Let your speech always be gracious, seasoned with salt, so that you may know how you ought to answer every one." Paul is using a distinction between "outsiders" and "insiders." By "outsiders" he means non-Christians. Are we to write them off as useless or treat them cavalierly? No. We are to treat them wisely and graciously. His concern is that Christians "make the most of the time" to draw others to the Lord by their good conduct and gracious speech.

We can relate better to others if we are wise about such differences. Where there is a shared understanding of and commitment to the Lord's ways, we can relate on the same level. It wouldn't be helpful, however, to expect everyone to approach difficulties the same way.

There are times when the approach we take with fellow Christians also produces good results with others. For example, if we speak directly about difficulties, some people will accept our approach and even be thankful for it.

I had several conversations with a man I knew who freely admitted that he was only a nominal Christian. He acknowledged that he wasn't particularly looking to the Lord to know how to do things. We had the occasion to discuss some serious matters in his life, and several times I respectfully, but directly, told him I thought his approaches weren't right in God's eyes. At the end of one of these discussions I said to him, "I hope you aren't upset with how I'm saying these things." He answered, "Far from it. I find it refreshing. You're the only one I know who will speak to me like this." Our direct conversations helped resolve some difficulties that the indirect approach could not.

Yet one of my Christian friends reported he had tried the same thing with a Christian co-worker without success.

> There was a man I worked with who would regularly break whatever agreements we established. That really made me frustrated. He was a Christian so I thought I could discuss the situation with him directly. I told him how I saw it. He was angry and said it wasn't fair for me to attack him. He didn't seem to be able to accept my attempts to better our relationship. So I decided I better not try to handle things that way in the future.

How can we tell when it would be good to speak about difficulties directly and when it wouldn't? There is no easy answer. We should be much more careful when we don't know what another person's response will be. We should be ready to change the direct approach when we find it bringing more difficulty than good. However, some situations may force us to take the direct approach. For example, we can't let serious sins go by. If we do take the direct approach, we should also be prepared to accept some possible negative consequences.

Nancy, who worked as a waitress, had serious

ongoing problems with her boss. She was not the only one: he expected waitresses to set the tables, take the orders and remember them without writing anything down, clean off the tables, take care of the cash register, and load the dishwasher. They would get frantic trying to do it all. The boss was also the cook and would frequently get the orders wrong and blame it on the waitresses.

Nancy told me, "This was where things really went wrong, because you couldn't prove anything to him since the orders weren't written down." Nancy was becoming frustrated and thought she would at least try to tell the boss why no one liked to work for him. It could cost her her job, but she thought it should be done anyway. When she tried to talk to the boss he wouldn't accept anything she was saying, and he fired her.

Nancy was probably right not to let the problem go. Although she lost her job, she had prepared herself for that to happen and was confident she could find another. In a similar situation someone else who could not withstand the loss of a job may need to adapt to a misguided boss. The key is to determine ahead of time to accept whatever negative consequences might come.

Another area in which to be careful is asking others for forgiveness. It can be helpful in some cases but not in others.

A young Christian woman named Diane was

living in an apartment with her sister Karen. Diane became a Christian and shortly afterwards learned to seek forgiveness when she had wronged others. She soon found out Karen didn't want to approach things that way. When Diane did something wrong she would ask Karen's forgiveness. But Karen just became more irritated each time. Karen wanted to handle wrongdoing by simply forgetting about it. Diane realized she would just be making the relationship worse if she persisted in asking forgiveness. Karen wasn't at the point where she could accept that.

Another young woman got involved with a Christian group when she went away from home to study at a university. She also learned about asking others to forgive her when she did something wrong. Once, when she was back home visiting her parents, she got into an argument with her mother and stormed out of the room. Later, when she had cooled down, she realized she had acted wrongly and went to her mother and asked her, in the presence of her father, to forgive her. Her parents were so shocked that they didn't know what to say at first. A conversation started, though, in which they did forgive her but also asked her forgiveness for several things they had done wrong in the past. There was a significant improvement in their relationship from that time on.

If people are ready to approach relationships the way that Christ teaches, then a great deal of good can result. But if they are not ready to do that, we should relate to them in a way they can receive. We need wisdom and sensitivity to know when and how to point out their wrongs and when to repent of our own wrongs.

Howard and Bob, two Christian men I know, work at the same place. They told me the following story of some difficulties they had on their job.

Bob was always getting into arguments with one of their co-workers. If it wasn't politics, it was company policy, or perhaps religion. The co-worker was not a Christian, but he claimed to be interested in what Howard and Bob believed. Still every conversation Bob had with him turned into an argument.

On the other hand, Howard was able to relate very well to the same man. Bob couldn't seem to do it. Howard once showed me a doodle that Bob had passed to him while their co-worker was arguing about Christianity. It was a picture of a heart carved out of stone and the words, "Why is he so hard-hearted?" The doodle was sad graphic evidence of Bob's failures to relate well.

Bob eventually asked Howard why he never had the same problem with their co-worker. He wondered what Howard's secret was.

TEN

Keeping Peace

WHEN THEIR CO-WORKER attacked Christianity, Bob always felt called on to defend it so convincingly that the other man was left with no choice but to agree. He felt vaguely guilty if he couldn't win all their arguments, and, of course, he couldn't.

The co-worker probably enjoyed arguing with Bob. But the arguments were fruitless, and Bob should have realized it was better to avoid them. It wasn't seriously wrong to argue, but it wasn't helpful.

Howard, on the other hand, actively avoided arguing with the other man. He would not pursue anything that might be a cause for contention. Howard had learned to implement a scriptural principle that Bob had never noticed before. Romans 12:18 says, "If possible, so far as it depends on you, live peaceably with all."

It isn't often that we find the scriptures teaching us to do something "if we can." Imagine the commandment, "If you can manage it, do not steal." Or, "See if you can't work it out to honor your father and your mother." Yet in Romans 12:18 Paul says, "If possible . . ."

Why the tentativeness? Because living in peace with others isn't entirely up to us. If the others involved in our relationships don't want to live peaceably with us, then the relationship is not peaceful. The relationship can't be peaceful if they are hostile. Jesus himself didn't live peacefully with all of the people of his time. In the end they put him to death. The lack of peace, however, did not start with him, but with us sinful men.

The Lord calls us to act the way he did. So far as it depends on us we are to live at peace with all. The passage refers primarily to relationships with non-Christians. We may have the same need to do all we can for peace with other Christians, but here Paul is concerned with teaching Christians how to relate with non-Christians. The supposition is that among Christians it should be possible to live in peace. But when people don't accept Christian ways, it may not always be possible. It is important not to approach our relationships with non-Christians as if they are always going to work out the same way as Christian relationships.

What do we do when people aren't ready for Christian ways? We have an example in how the Lord related to us when we weren't ready.

Romans 2:4 says, "Do you not know that God's kindness is meant to lead you to repentance?" When we needed to repent, God was kind to us. But he was kind to us so that we could come to repentance. He knows that the manifestation of his kindness can open us up to his grace so that we will turn away from wrong and come to him. When the Lord has to deal with people who are not in a good relationship with him, the qualities that he shows most are kindness, patience, and forbearance.

These qualities are more necessary when you are not in a committed relationship with someone. Where a commitment exists we can handle difficulties more directly. In a committed relationship the other person is less likely to see it as a personal attack. They can understand that it is an act of love when we bring up difficulties. It is an act of love because our purpose is to bring about a better relationship.

The Lord has called us to be men and women of peace. Our intention should always be to establish peace. We should "bend over backwards" for good relationships. We should make it a central concern in our lives and be willing to sacrifice for it.

Titus 3:1-5 contains similar direction. "Remind them . . . to avoid quarreling, to be gentle, and to show perfect courtesy toward all men. For we ourselves were once foolish, disobedient, led astray, slaves to various passions and pleasures, passing our days in malice and envy, hated by men and hating one another; but when the goodness and loving kindness of God our Savior appeared, he saved us, not because of deeds done by us in righteousness, but in virtue of his own mercy." God had mercy on us and so we are to have mercy on others.

This means we are also to approach others with a nonjudgmental attitude, which is not always easy. It's easier to judge others and think there's no excuse for their bad behavior. We have learned to act righteously, why shouldn't they? But we need to keep in mind that once we did no better. At one time we lived in foolishness and disobedience. We didn't get out of it by our own heroism but by God's grace. We experienced God's power and were given the grace to live in a different way. We are still growing in God's ways with the help of his Holy Spirit.

If we take the wrong attitude we end up making it harder for non-Christians. We came to the Lord's ways by his grace and forgiveness, and that will also be the way others come to a different life.

We should forbear and cooperate even with some unreasonable requests. We should look for ways to serve non-Christians. The passage also says, "Speak evil of no one." We shouldn't complain about others or be drawn into criticizing them. It's not that we're supposed to be weak or hesitant. Rather we're supposed to have an underlying peaceableness in our approach to other people. It's something that is important if we are going to represent the Lord as Christians.

Perhaps you've read C.S. Lewis's Chronicles of Narnia. In *The Voyage of the Dawn Treader,* which is my favorite in the series, we meet the incredibly creepy Eustace Clarence Scrubb. Some of the other characters, Edmund and Lucy and Prince Caspian, do an impressive job of putting up with him through the first half of the book. Reepicheep doesn't. Eventually, through his greed, Eustace gets turned into a dragon. (That's the kind of thing that happens in Narnia.) His life as a dragon is extremely lonely and gruesome, and he begins to repent. A key part in his changing is played by how well the others have previously treated him.

> He realised that he . . . wanted to be friends. He wanted to get back among humans and talk and laugh and share things. He realised he was a monster cut off from the whole human race. An appalling loneliness came over him. He began to see that the others had not really been fiends at all. He began to wonder if he himself had been such a nice person as he had always supposed. He longed for their voices. He would have been grateful for a kind word even from Reepicheep. . . .

> . . . Poor Eustace realised more and more that since the first day he came on board he had been an unmitigated nuisance.

The contrast between his own behavior and the peaceful behavior of the others became painfully clear to Eustace. Seeing the contrast made him want to be different, and that was all Aslan was waiting for. (In Narnia, a land of talking animals, Christ appears as the lion Aslan.) Brought to a sincere repentance by seeing the goodness of the others in contrast to his own despicable behavior, Eustace could now be helped to change. The great lion rips away the dragon's flesh and releases the restored Eustace who finally becomes a pleasant young man.

Lewis concludes the incident by saying, "It would be nice, and fairly nearly true, to say that 'from that time forth Eustace was a different boy.' To be strictly accurate, he began to be a different boy. He had relapses. There were still many days when he could be very tiresome. But most of those I shall not notice. The cure had begun."

The story of Eustace illustrates the positive effects of kindness. It was the steadfast kindness of his friends that motivated Eustace to want to change. And this doesn't happen just in storybooks.

A married woman I know related a similar story about her marriage. She had been a devout

Christian as she grew up, and her family had trained her to be a good mature woman. She married another Christian, which was very important to her. However, she found out as she lived with him that he was only a Christian in name. He lived mostly for himself and was both irresponsible and easily angered with her and the children.

Over several years of their marriage she had steadfastly responded to him with kindness and peace. Many times she felt like doing just the opposite. She was sustained in going on by many good Christian friendships. Eventually her husband realized how badly he was treating her and the children. He asked to get some help through her Christian friends. His own account of the matter went something like this.

"I always realized how awful I was being. Mary was so good, and I really appreciated that. I didn't want to yell at her and the kids. I hated myself every time I did. But that didn't help. Year after year she was faithful to me and even kind to me. I've had enough. Please help me." With the help of other Christians he has become a good, responsible husband. Like Eustace, he's not yet perfect, but the cure has begun.

Sometimes the Lord puts us in situations that call for heroic forbearance. "You have heard that it was said, 'An eye for an eye and a tooth for a tooth.' But I say to you, Do not resist one who is evil. But if any one strikes you on the right cheek, turn to him the other also; and if any one would sue you and take your coat, let him have your cloak as well; and if any one forces you to go one mile, go with him two miles" (Mt 5:38-41).

We should be like the Lord who is patient and merciful. He disciplines his children because he is concerned that they reach full maturity. But his first concern with them was to make them his children. Similarly, we should be more patient with those who aren't Christians, because the first thing they need is to form a relationship with the Lord. We should put up with many things from them that we would not necessarily accept from other Christians.

Several years ago a pastor who was a friend of mine was caring for a young man named Joe, a hospital orderly. Joe's relationship with his immediate supervisor was getting worse and worse, but Joe could not figure out why. There were some small things that she did that irritated him, but he was sure they weren't all that important. Yet he found himself day after day acting worse toward her. At the same time this was not consistent with his behavior at home or with other people. It wasn't like him to be in conflict with people. Just the opposite, he was pleasant and quite easy to get along with. His partner suggested forbearance.

"Forbearance? There's hardly anything to

forbear, and still I can't do it. She's not all that bad."

"Is it that you resent working under the direction of a woman?"

"No. I've regularly had women for supervisors. Orderlies frequently do. That has never been a problem for me. It's not really any problem now either."

"Well, I don't know what else to say. All I can tell you is to pray for a solution. Maybe you should ask the Lord to change your attitude. If you persistently seek his help, I'm sure it will come. Let me know what happens."

The next week the problem was even worse. In this case God was going to answer Joe's prayers in a different way than Joe expected.

ELEVEN

Knowing Your Limits

IT TOOK A WHILE to get to the bottom of Joe's problem. It turned out that the difficulty he was having started because the supervisor was expecting him to take part in abortions. He knew that abortion was wrong, but he thought his responsibility to his job justified taking part in them. He went along with the abortions, but he felt constantly guilty about it.

As a result Joe was left with an internal conflict that was expressed in his bad relationship with his supervisor. She was expecting him to do something that he was convinced was wrong. Every contact with her reminded him of the problem. He acted badly towards her without understanding why.

As he talked about it with his pastor, Joe saw that he should not participate in abortions. Loyalty to his employer did not extend beyond his faithfulness to God's law. He decided not to take part in the operations anymore.

When he went to talk to his supervisor, he

finally found it easy to deal with her. He was now sure of himself and could tell her his position calmly and clearly. A short while later he was fired from his job. He had realized before talking to his supervisor that that would probably be the outcome. In the time between talking to her and losing his job his relationship with her worked very well. He was no longer irritable and unreasonable. Once he was doing the right thing, he was at peace with himself and could relate peacefully with her.

Deciding ahead of time the limit to which we will cooperate with others is a key to being able to relate well. The time of conflict and crisis is not a good time for making a hard decision. By then it's usually too late. When we're in the midst of a difficult situation and don't know what our limits are, we feel cornered and we tend to react badly.

Christians need to know what is right and wrong in many situations. Many difficulties come from the fact that we don't know what is right and wrong in situations that we face. We end up with internal conflicts and therefore respond poorly. We need Christian teaching to help us decide what's right and wrong, what is in accordance with the way of life Christ has given us.

During one of the summers between my college years I was rooming with another Christian man named Mike who was a few years older than me. Another young man with whom we had made acquaintance had no place to stay. He did not share our Christian convictions, but he was in need. He was without a job and had no place to go. We invited him to stay with us until he found work.

One day I was surprised to come home and find out he had taken a girl to bed with him in the middle of the afternoon. I felt completely confused because I didn't know what to say. I knew what he had done was wrong, but on the other hand we had taken him in out of concern for his need. I was torn inside. Was a Christian supposed to put up with something like this because the call to charity was higher? I didn't know what to do. But it was clear that he thought his behavior was acceptable, and he wasn't open to hearing another point of view.

When my roommate came home and heard what had happened, he handled the situation decisively. He immediately threw our guest out. Clearly and firmly, without loosing control of himself, he informed our guest that he was no longer welcome. "That is not the kind of behavior we permit in this house." The guest was gone as soon as he could gather his things.

Of course, there is room for repentance from any kind of wrongdoing, no matter how serious. But our guest was not willing to consider repentance. The greater charity for our guest was not to approve what he was doing indirectly by allowing him to stay. There was also no way of telling what he would do in the future. We were not responsible to track him down and see that everything he did was right, but we were responsible for what happened in our own house.

I was thankful for my roommate's clarity of mind. If I had understood ahead of time what was right for a Christian to do in such a case, I would have been prepared for handling the situation without so much internal conflict.

At other times there is no clear right or wrong in a situation of difficulty. In those cases it often helps to make agreements with people about what we are willing to do or what we expect them to do. With the agreement in place both people know how they should handle themselves. How we should respond is determined by the agreement.

Once a young woman named Kathy was staying with my family when we lived in an apartment building. Any sound above the level of normal conversation carried easily through the walls. The people in the apartment next to this woman's bedroom frequently played loud rock music on their stereo. Most of the time it didn't matter because Kathy was away at her job. The little time in the evenings that she spent in her room was often accompanied by the sound of rock music from the neighboring apartment. Kathy didn't like the music but she tolerated it.

Once the neighbors' stereo was playing late into the night. Kathy tried to sleep for about an hour but just couldn't do it. My wife and I had not turned in for the night, and she came down and told us her predicament. I decided to go to the next apartment and ask them to turn off the stereo so she could sleep. The entrance to their apartment was on the other side of the building and consequently I had never met the neighbors.

The people in the other apartment were very accommodating and happy to turn off the stereo. I returned to our apartment. Kathy went back to bed, but all of a sudden the music started louder than before. She came down again and now we, too, could hear the music loudly in every room. Over and over the words pounded out, "I think it's so groovy now, that people are finally getting together." All of us were confused, and Kathy was pretty discouraged.

Suddenly it dawned on me what was probably going on. The neighbors were sending us a peace message contained in the lyrics of the song: "I think it's so groovy now, that people are finally getting together." After the song was finished there was no more music for the rest of the night. Our neighbors had simply been trying to communicate peace in their own way.

Shortly after that incident my wife and I moved to our first house and had our first child, Samuel. The window of the only bedroom Samuel could sleep in was just twenty feet away from the window of an apartment in the next house. The young man who lived in the neighboring apartment played in a rock band. He would regularly have the other members of the band over to his apartment to practice their music. Because of the summer heat they needed the window open and so did our son. Twenty feet isn't very far away from loudspeakers when a rock band is playing. Something had to be done or our son was never going to sleep.

I went over to try to talk to them about our difficulty, and we settled on a simple solution. We agreed on times when our son could sleep without the music and when he would be awake so they could feel free to play. But the next night at Samuel's bedtime, when they had agreed to keep things quiet, the band was just starting to practice again. This time the music was not a message of peace.

I went over to talk to them again. It happened that their landlady was in front of their house working on the yard as I went in. I greeted her as I passed by. I knocked at their door. Again they were open to settling the problem. They had simply forgotten what was agreed the night before. (Remember what I said about agreements being broken in chapter 5.) They immediately stopped and never played at the wrong time again.

As I walked out the landlady was flabbergasted. She couldn't imagine what I had done to get them to stop playing. She couldn't understand how anyone could get young people to stop playing rock music. What I had done was nothing earthshaking. It wasn't my personal dynamism or imposing authority that resolved the problem. I had simply explained our difficulty and need and proposed an agreement that they found acceptable. Often that is all that is needed to bring peace.

Assertiveness training is popular today. People are taught to assert themselves to get what they want. As a method of conflict resolution, assertiveness is inadequate. It fails to take into account the concerns and the assertive power of others. The person who relies on self-assertiveness may settle conflicts, but he does it in a way that damages his relationships with others rather than building them up.

The simple approach of making agreements works much better. The needs of both parties are addressed. Once the matter is settled, it won't repeatedly arise in an ongoing battle of self-assertions.

But should we expect that all disagreements we have with others can be resolved by making agreements? What happens when an agreement cannot be reached?

Before I try to answer those questions, let me

tell you about something that happened to me while I was at college. For several years I studied art and developed close friendships with several other art students and teachers. The teacher whom I regarded as the best on the faculty told me he thought I was his most promising student. He had a great interest in my development.

During this same period of time I was becoming increasingly committed as a Christian through another set of friends. My two groups of friends didn't know each other, and as the months passed I realized I couldn't give enough time to both of them. Eventually I began to take more courses that directly furthered my deepening interest in Christianity. I still took some art courses, but it was obvious to my friends among the art students and faculty that I was no longer involved with them in the same way.

The teacher who had been interested in me lamented the change. I didn't like disappointing him, but I was sure of the direction I was choosing. He thought I was making a big mistake.

TWELVE

Separate If Necessary

MY INVOLVEMENT with the group of artists gradually began to lessen. Before another year was over, most of them were surpassing me in their ability to draw and paint because they were still putting all their time into art. I was not able to be completely with them in spirit, since I was choosing to put my priority on the Christian work of the other group.

The teacher who had been interested in me had hoped for a lot. Now he began to invest himself more in other students. I didn't like disappointing him, but I was sure of the direction I was choosing. My decision was not a matter of following God's commandments about sin and righteousness. It was a matter of choosing one good thing over another.

I never lost those friends though. I've had contact with some of them over the years and even shared work on some art projects with them. The separation was not total. Our paths diverged profoundly, yet it was not a matter of animosity or of an ultimate break.

Sometimes others accept the decisions we make as Christians, and sometimes they do not. Or perhaps, like my friends in art school, they accept our decisions but remain disappointed. In other situations people may expect us to compromise our faith. If that happens, we may need to separate from them in a way that does not work smoothly. Such separations, however, do not necessarily have to be complete or permanent.

I once met a young man named Marty. We had some of the same classes, and we lived near one another. We began to spend time together. We were once walking past a record store when to my surprise Marty said, "Is there any record you want? I could steal it for you." I liked him and I hated to offend him, yet I could not agree to what he was proposing. I stammered out some kind of refusal that I don't even recall now.

One evening we were out again and Marty proposed doing some vandalism. Again, since I felt we had a good friendship, it was hard for me to say no, but that was what I had to do.

Some similar incidents followed. I was starting to see that our friendship would be shortlived. Although we remained friendly, I had to decide to stop spending time with him. I don't know if Marty ever did the kinds of things he suggested to me, but our friendship ended because I had to separate from the wrong things he was asking me to be involved in.

Christians tend to think it's never right to separate. Separation, however, need not be a bad thing, or indicate a lack of love. It is often an expression of love.

You may recall that Abraham's loyalty to God called for him to separate from others in several instances. First of all he was called to leave Ur and go to the land of Canaan. To follow God he had to leave his homeland and go to another part of the world. After arriving in Canaan he had to separate from his nephew Lot. "Lot, who went with Abram, also had flocks and herds and tents, so that the land could not support both of them dwelling together, . . . and there was strife between the herdsmen of Abram's cattle and the herdsmen of Lot's cattle. . . .

"Then Abram said to Lot, 'Let there be no strife between you and me, and between your herdsmen and my herdsmen; for we are kinsmen. Is not the whole land before you? Separate yourself from me. If you take the left hand, then I will go to the right; or if you take the right hand, then I will go to the left.' . . . So Lot chose for himself all the Jordan valley, and Lot journeyed east; thus they separated from each other. Abram dwelt in the land of Canaan, while Lot dwelt among the cities of the valley" (Gn 13:5-6, 8-9, 11).

In the next chapter of Genesis, Lot was taken captive, along with all his family and possessions, by Chedorlaomer. When Abram heard the news he mustered his men, attacked Chedorlaomer, and freed Lot. Out of loyalty, Abram went out to battle, risking life and resources for Lot's sake. Separation had been necessary for their herdsmen to live in peace, but it was not an end to their relationship or to Abram's loyalty to Lot.

Later, after God had changed his name, Abraham again demonstrated his loyalty to Lot. God revealed to Abraham that he intended to destroy Sodom and Gomorrah where Lot was living. At risk to himself, Abraham interceded with God and Lot's life was spared. Genesis 19:29 says "So it was that, when God destroyed the cities of the valley, God remembered Abraham, and sent Lot out of the midst of the overthrow, when he overthrew the cities in which Lot dwelt." God did not regard the separation between Abraham and Lot as an indication of a bad relationship. Rather he saved Lot's life because of Abraham's loyalty.

Some separations that we should undertake as Christians may be more radical than this case. Still, the separation should not be made with animosity. Separation simply means that at this time and place it doesn't make sense to keep on working or living in the same close relationship.

Some degree of separation is better for everyone involved.

There are many reasons for choosing separation. Christians need to be prepared to follow the right direction even if some separation is involved. This doesn't mean neglecting other duties. For example, Jesus rebuked the Pharisees and the scribes for neglecting their duty to care for their parents when they had separated from them for the sake of religious duties. They claimed that what would normally have been given to their parents was now "given to God." The Pharisees and scribes should have served God without neglecting their parents (Mk 7:9-13).

Sometimes separation may be necessary to avoid wrongdoing. That was the situation I faced when my friend proposed shoplifting and vandalism. Other situations may simply involve circumstances that in themselves are neither right nor wrong, but staying in the situation makes the conflict worse. Such was the case of Abraham and Lot whose great possessions were too much for the land they shared.

Christians I know have been involved in many kinds of situations that called for separation. Bill had to stop selling vacuum cleaners because the sales techniques he was required to use took advantage of low-income families. Tom was fired when he wouldn't steal lumber for his boss from a neighboring construction site. Greg moved out of his university housing when the other men in his apartment began to have women live with them. Lois left her sales clerk job when the store began to sell pornography. Valerie's friendship with Carol ended when Carol began to encourage other women to get abortions. Paula was disowned by her father when she became a Christian. Jeff moved his family to another side of town when his son got involved with a bad group of companions.

Separation can also happen within a group of Christians, though it is usually more limited and temporary.

A young woman named Ellen whose parents had died was invited to move in with a Christian family. For reasons no one could understand at the time, Ellen soon felt rejected and mistreated by the family. There didn't seem to be any right or wrong in the situation. An alternative housing possibility with another family turned up. It seemed best for Ellen to move and temporarily separate from the first family. After another year of Christian growth Ellen had changed quite a bit. She now saw that the problem with the first family had been hers. She had been too self-concerned and sensitive about very small things. The year of growth had brought her to a new level of maturity, and she was able to restore her friendship with the first family.

Separation can also be misused. A young man named David who was studying at a university became a Christian but found that his parents were not at all pleased with his conversion. They were professed atheists and thought he was making a big mistake with his life. Whenever David was at home they attacked him for his new beliefs and serious arguments would follow. David wanted to go home less and less. He was already paying his own way through school, and he knew he could support himself. It would be harder to be independent from his parents but he could do it.

David decided to inform his parents he would be coming home only rarely. He knew he treated them badly in response to their attacks, but he thought there was no solution but separation. David asked me for advice, and I told him I thought he was making a mistake. He was not yet aware of another area of the Lord's teaching.

THIRTEEN

Conflicts with Authorities

DAVID WAS IN A CONFLICT with his parents. Even if they were not Christians, they had authority over him as parents that should have affected how he related to them.

What is the difference between a conflict with a peer and a conflict with someone who has authority over us? This sort of situation can occur in families, on our jobs, or with government authorities. How should David have acted?

A basic principle of the Lord's teaching goes against our natural tendencies in this area. We are inclined to relate to people as their own behavior seems to deserve. If they act in a good way, we respond in a good way. If they act badly, we respond badly to them. We absolve ourselves from any guilt because we think they deserve what they are getting.

What the Lord wants from us is different. He teaches us always to relate to people according to our new Christian nature. Even if they mistreat us we are still to treat them well. "Bless those who persecute you; bless and do not curse them. . . . Repay no one evil for evil, but take thought for what is noble in the sight of all. . . . Do not be overcome by evil, but overcome evil with good" (Rom 12:14, 17, 21). David should have continued to act respectfully to his parents even if he had reason to believe that they were mistreating him.

To put this principle a different way, we are always supposed to relate well to others, not adjusting our actions according to how well they behave. David accepted that what he had been doing was not what God wanted. He began to respond in a better way to his parents, even though they wanted to influence him not to be a Christian. In the intervening years his change in approach has had a profound effect. His parents still disagree with Christianity, but they have stopped putting pressure on David about it. He has frequently taken Christian friends home to visit. His parents have been surprised at how much they like his friends, and they are glad to have them as guests. David still hopes that his parents will open up to Christ, but his good behavior has already brought peace in a situation that would otherwise have ended in a bitter separation.

Christians act respectfully toward authority

because it is God who has established authority. Paul says, "There is no authority except from God, and those that exist have been instituted by God. Therefore he who resists the authorities resists what God has appointed, and those who resist will incur judgment" (Rom 13:1-2).

People who hold positions of authority don't necessarily know their authority comes from God. The Roman leaders in Paul's time, who were idolators, did not see themselves as established in authority by the God of the Israelites. But to Paul it was not relevant whether they knew it or not, or whether they were personally righteous or not. As a rule they weren't. Paul didn't say they were to be accepted as authorities only if their lives passed the test of righteousness, but because they participated in an order that ultimately stemmed from God. Therefore, Christians needed to respect them and relate to them as real authorities.

The Roman leaders were not spiritual authorities. Submitting to them was not a matter of inner abandonment of the heart in the sense that we should give ourselves over to God. The same thing is true of civil authorities today. We can't count on them in all cases to stand for truth and righteousness. Sometimes they will, and sometimes they won't. But they are still in positions of authority, and we should accept their authority.

There are different kinds of authority and no one in authority is granted by God the right to handle all matters. Our obedience to civil authorities, for example, is not absolute. We obey them only in matters that they govern. We do not need to assent if they demand things from us that are against God's laws.

The same is true for family and job authorities. David, the young man I mentioned earlier, was right to continue as a Christian even though his parents did not agree with him. He was wrong, however, to treat his parents badly.

The book of Acts records that the apostles were put in prison because the authorities wanted to stop them from evangelizing. God miraculously released them, and they began to preach again. Then they were brought before the authorities and sternly reminded that they were forbidden to teach about Jesus. Peter boldly responded, "We must obey God rather than men" (Acts 5:17-29).

Peter was not exalting his own position over that of the authorities. Today there are many people who consider it honorable and courageous to challenge authority in any way. But that is not what Peter was doing. He accepted that the Jewish leaders had a rightful authority from God. He was not putting himself above them or saying he had a better idea than they did. He opposed them in this case only because the Lord, whose authority was higher than theirs, had given a different command. Peter was remaining in submission to authority, not exalting himself above it.

We relate to authority respectfully because it is God who has established authority. It may appear to us that we are most often relating to authorities better than they deserve. Whether that is the case or not, God expects us to heed his word and respond to authority in a good way. We will be examined on how well we do. The person in authority will also be examined on how well he conducts himself in his position of authority.

Man is created under the authority of a God who is the Master of creation. Man is not a master of himself. In reality, if we set ourselves outside the authority of God, our rightful Master, we become slaves of another master who is God's enemy. We may think we are becoming our own master, but it is Satan who takes us captive. This is what happened in the fall, when Adam and Eve stepped outside the authority of God, they stepped outside the grace of God and under the power of Satan. Don't forget that authority is a basic issue. It is so basic that it was the issue over which our shared human history took a turn for the worse at the beginning.

In sum, we owe respect, honor, and obedience to people who are over us in government, on our jobs, and in our families. Whether they are Christians or not, they have real authority.

Many of us need to undergo a basic conversion on this point. I realized some years ago that I did not obey most authorities freely but out of compulsion. I would just as soon have been free of them, but since they were there I would obey as far as I had to. I pushed everything I could get away with to the limit. I am sure this attitude spilled over to my relationship with God. I remained obedient to God, but my obedience was focused on staying within the limits. Consequently the more personal aspects of a relationship with God were lacking in my life. I had less sense of God as my loving Father and less confidence in his provision for me. I knew I ought to obey God but I was closer to his laws than I was to God himself.

A reluctant attitude towards authority says, "I would be better off without authority." It's not true. God is in authority, and I came to realize I was better off to submit to his authority, and to the human authorities he has established, than I would be without them. Obedience should come not only out of fear of punishment but also out of an interior conversion and submission to rightful authority. I should remain well within the limits set by authority and not stand at the borderline trying to push the edge farther and farther out.

I once got a speeding ticket by pushing the limits too far. Early one morning I was driving back from a vacation and there was almost no traffic. The roads seemed open and safe. I had an inkling that I was not pleasing God, but I wasn't ready to surrender my desire to arrive at my destination quickly.

When the police radar caught me, I at first excused myself. A driver in front of me had been weaving. It seemed safer to speed by him rather than risk getting hit while passing more slowly. My first reaction was defensive. I felt I was being ticketed for trying to protect myself. But then I realized I had been pushing at the edges of what God wanted. If I hadn't been speeding in the first place there would have been no reason to pass the other car.

But it is also helpful to realize that laws do not always clearly define our responsibilities. For example, there may be some unclarity in tax laws that leaves us not knowing for sure what we owe. At other times laws are qualified by how they are enforced. In many places the speed limits are enforced with some leeway. Sometimes the authorities allow traffic to go a bit over the limit. Then it may be wise to drive at the speed of the flow of traffic, especially if traffic is heavy. Rigidly keeping under the limit may be dangerous because everyone else is going faster. A slower car gets in the way. However, the basic point still stands. We should accept the laws as they are set by those in authority. In a given case, perhaps we should fit into the flow of traffic as it is enforced by the authorities. But that is very different from always pushing the law to its limit.

We all need to make the basic conversion to obeying authorities out of freedom instead of out of compulsion. Pushing to the edge of what's allowed is a sign that we are obeying out of compulsion. We'd rather be free of the authority and do what we want. It would be better to freely submit to authority first. If we do freely submit, we are more able to understand what might be legitimate exceptions. If our basic intent is to abide by the direction of authority, life will work differently than if our intent is to get away with everything we can.

Conflicts with family authorities may also arise for Christians. One common problem occurs when family members have a hard time accepting the changes that follow when one of them comes to a new Christian commitment.

The person who has become a Christian is frequently surprised to find out that the other family members are not overjoyed with what has happened to him. He is so happy with the change in his life that he presumes the others will be too. But he should realize they will probably need to be won over to an acceptance of the change.

Don and Carole were joyful new Christians, but their high-school-aged children wondered what had come over them. They picked up a book on how Christian parents should raise their children and naively thought the children would gladly accept the improved approach. But it didn't happen that way. The children weren't at all sure they wanted their parents to be talking to them about Christianity and watching over their activities more closely. What had seemed to them to be a normal parent-child relationship turned bitter overnight.

Don realized it wasn't working. He talked the situation over with Carole, and they settled on a new approach. They needed not only to change how they were relating to their children, but they also needed to win them to the change. They arranged for their children to meet some Christian university students who began to take the children to attractive Christian youth activities. Don began to invite his son to things he hadn't thought to invite him to before, like his hunting trips. Carole took their two daughters out to lunch weekly and began to establish a new closeness that hadn't existed before. The children slowly opened up to Christianity and finally agreed it was a real improvement for the family life.

Don and Carole did not give up just because their children resisted at first. As Christians they were still responsible to bring their family into God's plan. What they learned was that they could not simply command the change. They needed to win their children to it. Children who come to a new Christian commitment also frequently need to learn how to win their parents to seeing the change as something good.

Within families, changing to new Christian patterns of relating is often difficult. Expectations of immediate change often give way to discouragement because of past difficulties and deeply-rooted habits. Guilt or resentment over past wrongs and anxiety about the future can hinder our freedom to change. We should take such difficulties in stride and patiently work towards improvement.

No matter how serious her resolution to be respectful to her mother, Jane found herself falling back into disrespectful speech patterns whenever she visited her parents. She was now married and living a good Christian family life with her husband and two daughters. She thought the way she behaved when she visited her parents was a sign that her Christianity wasn't worth much. Her husband, Tim, encouraged her to be more patient about changing. Yes, she did the wrong thing, but from his more objective perspective he could see that she was improving. Putting away discouragement helped her a great deal. The periods of good relating increased and the number of flare-ups decreased. Jane's not perfect yet, but a big improvement came when she realized that the long history of bad relating made the problem harder to solve.

Another kind of problem can occur when older children are confused about what matters still call for obedience to their parents.

Laura knew her parents weren't happy that she was involved with a Christian group. She still lived at home, but they felt they were losing her, that they were in competition with her new Christian friends. Nothing was said directly, but Laura felt guilty because she could tell her parents were displeased.

Laura's problem was eventually solved. She found out that her parents didn't oppose her Christian involvement in itself. They were put at peace when she assured them that she would still be faithful to family time and to the things they felt were necessary for her life. They needed to know clearly where she stood in relationship to the family and their overall concern for her.

As children grow older, many family difficulties can be avoided by the use of clear agreements. If both the parents and children know what obedience and family participation is expected, they can relate with confidence. Normally more obedience and family participation will be needed if the children are still living at home than if they have moved out to live somewhere else.

What if the parents and children can't seem to agree? Are the children being inconsiderate of their parents? Should they more readily accede to their parents' wishes? Or are the parents perhaps expecting too much?

Some children feel their parents demand too much of their time. Rather than always accepting or rejecting an invitation, children should propose times to spend together before the parents have to ask them. The children should be thinking about what would make the relationship work well and taking initiative to get it to happen. Then the parents will know that the children want the relationship instead of feeling like they are avoiding it. I am not recommending that family time be considered the responsibility of the children, but that children who take initiative in their relationship with their parents avoid the tensions that arise when parents feel like their children aren't interested in them.

Other authority problems occur in employer-employee relationships. Employers who have a serious commitment to the Lord are sometimes confused about how they should treat those who work for them. Certainly they shouldn't be tyrants on the job, yet it would be a mistake for them to become too lenient because they think they are supposed to overlook wrongdoing. Christianity may better their working relationships, but it is not meant to make them a soft touch.

What about employees? The New Testament passages on slaves and masters state some principles that help resolve various kinds of conflicts that employees may encounter.

Colossians 3:22-24 says, "Slaves, obey in everything those who are your earthly masters, not with eyeservice, as men-pleasers, but in singleness of heart, fearing the Lord. Whatever your task, work heartily, as serving the Lord and not men, knowing that from the Lord you will receive the inheritance as your reward; you are serving the Lord Christ."

As in other authority relationships the principle here is that we serve those over us, not according to how they treat us, but according to how the Lord wants us to treat them. Everything in our life is a service to God. Therefore, we are faithful and obedient to our employers because we are serving God.

A young Christian woman I know encountered a difficult situation with her employer. Cindy worked as a secretary for the president of a company, who greatly depended on her. She was qualified to handle a heavy load of work and even to perform tasks beyond those normally expected of a secretary. When the president was away from the office on business for weeks at a time, she was able to direct the company successfully.

At a certain point, however, her boss began to have an affair with another woman. He began to ask Cindy to help him keep it hidden from his wife. Eventually she had to resign from her job because she couldn't cooperate with his adultery. Her boss was doubly offended with her for leaving. First of all, he genuinely needed her help on the job. Secondly, he was displeased with the obvious rebuke of his sinful behavior.

When Cindy was applying at a new company, they contacted her previous boss for an evaluation. He sent a letter slandering her, saying she was rarely on time for work and that her work was unacceptable. The letter was a serious threat to her chances of being employed again.

She was asked to phone her former boss for the transfer of some additional information about insurance and taxes. Since Cindy was a Christian, she had always acted respectfully to her employer. But now she was angry at him for slandering her. She wondered whether she would be able to control her anger during the phone call.

FOURTEEN

Imitate Christ, Not the World

AS A CHRISTIAN, Cindy needed to respond to her former boss according to Christ's teaching and not according to the way he had treated her. She knew it would be hard, but she determined to remain respectful. This was not the time to rebuke him for adultery; her leaving her job had already rebuked him. She did, however, intend to say respectfully that his slanderous letter was wrong.

Cindy called him on the phone. She managed to ask calmly for the information the new company needed to receive. Her former boss told her he understood the request, but then he pretended the phone connection was so bad that he had to hang up. That was the end of it. Cindy didn't have a chance to say anything more.

A few days later Cindy was surprised to find out she had been quickly accepted for the new job. The man who hired her had been able to read between the lines and understand that her former boss was unfairly out to get her. He had simply disregarded the obviously bitter letter.

Cindy never knew how her response affected her former boss. But when we respond to others in conflict situations according to what is right in the Lord, and not just according to how we have been treated, it often makes a significant difference to them.

I've lived in a university town for over ten years and known many students and several landlords. The students and the landlords always seem to be fighting. One year the students form organizations to withhold rent payments from the landlords. The next year the landlords raise rents or sue the city because they think the housing code is too strict and expensive. I've observed that the principle of responding in a good way, even in the midst of difficulty, makes a big difference for Christian students and their landlords.

Several young Christian women I knew were renting a house. One of them, Chris, accidentally started a grease fire while cooking. It was an old, wooden house, and the fire spread rapidly. By the time the firemen arrived, there had already been extensive damage to the kitchen. At least the women had managed to keep the fire from spreading to other rooms of the house. In the next few days Chris arranged for her father and several other young men from her church to rebuild everything that was damaged. The repairs were quickly done, and the landlord was impressed.

Later on I was looking for a house to rent, and Chris told her landlord about me. He had a house I liked, and he gladly rented it to me. As I talked with the landlord I realized how difficult it was to be a landlord in our town. He was seriously considering getting out of the business because it was so difficult to deal with the poor condition in which most of the students left houses.

"But," he told me, "every time I rent to those people Chris knows they leave my apartments in better condition than they were before. With other people I have to count on a big investment to restore the apartment before I can rent it again. I can see her group sure has high ideals."

What he said struck me because I knew the difference was not high ideals. Chris's Christian friends came from the same backgrounds that his other student tenants did. As human beings they weren't any different. The difference was that they had taken on a serious commitment to Christianity and had grown in the character of Christ. It was their commitment to Christ that made them different. What he was observing, without knowing it, was men and women of peace, who sought positive, good relationships. They did not take advantage of others or try to shirk their responsibilities. They tried to do all they could to build and keep good relationships because they knew that was what the Lord wanted.

As Christians we are called to demonstrate, not just believe, that the strength of God is greater than the power of evil. "Do not be overcome by evil, but overcome evil with good" (Rom 12:21) is one of the main teachings of the New Testament about how Christians should relate to those who do not share the Christian faith. Paul is saying that it is the nature of the world that we will experience a lot of evil. But the power and goodness of God working in us is supposed to overcome evil.

The alternative is to be overcome by the evil of the world around us, to be caught up in the same ways of behaving that others follow. If someone comes at us mad as a hornet, we tend to react like a nest of hornets: an eye for an eye and a tooth for a tooth. Or worse yet, we may pay back more evil than we receive, like Lamech who boasted that if wrong were done to him he would repay it seventy-seven times over (Gn 4:24).

As Christians we are not supposed to act like that, but to take the Lord as our model. Paul says, "Bless those who persecute you; bless and do not curse them. . . . Repay no one evil for evil" (Rom 12:14, 17). We are to remain firm in doing good and even make progress in the midst of evil. "And let us not grow weary in well-doing, for in due season we shall reap, if we do not lose heart. So then, as we have opportunity, let us do good to all men" (Gal 6:9-10). The Lord is calling us to be so persistently good that we replace evil with his grace. He wants us to be the kind of people who don't just accept things as they are but change them for the better.

One of my favorite Peanuts cartoons shows an angry Lucy approaching Snoopy. She chews him out and stands glaring at him, waiting for his response. He kisses her ever so sweetly and she is instantly changed, her anger melted away by his display of affection. Then Snoopy quotes the Proverb: "A soft answer turns away wrath" (Prv 15:1).

It's true. A kind response has great power to overcome evil. There is a basic issue in life for us. Will we be formed by the bad behavior around us, or will we have the inner spiritual strength to act differently, to act according to Christ's ways?

I lived for several years in another country where most of the drivers were extremely aggressive. For a long time I fought back in the same way. If another driver tried to beat me out, I tried just as hard to beat him out. If he cut too close in front of me, I flashed my brights at him. Of course, that didn't increase road safety for anyone.

One day another American who was also a Christian picked me up for a luncheon appointment. I was amazed by how calmly he drove. He let the aggressive drivers have their way and still did just fine in getting around the city. His example opened my eyes to how I had been acting. I realized I had slipped into shaping my actions by what others were doing instead of by how God wanted me to act. I made a decision to change. After that I enjoyed driving a lot more, and I realized how much safer it was for me on the roads.

It is a great freedom for us to imitate Christ. The models the world around us presents do not match up to the model of our Master.

But can we be victorious in every conflict? Even Christ in his perfection was not free from conflict. Is imitating Christ and following his teaching enough to bring us through every conflict in the right way?

FIFTEEN

A Final Word

MANY OF THE CONFLICTS we experience are very serious. In some cases they have a grave outcome. Christ's solutions, taught in scripture, bring wonderful results. At times, however, someone involved in a conflict is not willing to take steps towards a resolution. Nor is help from mature Christians who are skilled in guiding people always available.

At the beginning of this book I quoted the diary of Mary Richardson Walker, a Christian woman who did not have the help she needed to deal with the difficulties between her and her husband. If there had been someone to guide them, their Christian lives could have been very different. How should we approach conflicts when we don't seem to have the help we need?

Sigrid Undset's novel *Kristin Lavransdatter* tells the story of a woman in such a situation. She disregards the wisdom of her parents and enters a very difficult marriage. Her life is filled with hardship, and her husband dies, leaving many conflicts with Kristin and others unresolved.

When Kristin herself reaches the time of her own death, she is given grace from God to see that he still was working to bring good out of all the hardships in her life. She realizes that God "had seen the sin and sorrow, the love and hate.... and he had descended; his feet had trodden the peopled lands, and stood in palaces and in huts; he had gathered up the sorrows and the sins of rich and poor, and lifted them aloft with him upon a cross." She realizes that he came precisely to forgive the sins and heal the wounds. "It seemed to her to be a mystery that she could not fathom, but which she knew most surely none the less, that God held her fast in a covenant made for her without her knowledge by a love poured out upon her richly—and in despite of her self-will, in despite of her heavy, earthbound spirit, somewhat of this love had become *part* of her."

God gives wisdom for handling conflicts. Where we can apply it, it gives life. Where some trials of life remain, we can still depend on God's promises. We can still seek his wisdom and his help. We can have the faith that he is in control and knows our needs. When and how he will answer our prayers is not as clear as the certainty that he will answer them. And he will answer them to a greater degree than we could imagine possible. He has promised to lead the followers of his Son to a time when he will make all things new, when "he will wipe away every tear from their eyes, and death shall be no more, neither shall there be mourning nor crying nor pain any more" (Rv 21:4).

The Living as a Christian Series

Basic Christian Maturity
Growing in Faith
Steve Clark
Knowing God's Will
Steve Clark
Decision to Love
Ken Wilson
God First
Ken Wilson
Sons and Daughters of God
Ken Wilson
Growing Closer to God
Tom Gryniewicz
Person to Person
Jim Berlucchi

Overcoming Obstacles to Christian Living
How to Repair the Wrong You've Done
Ken Wilson
Getting Free
Bert Ghezzi
Handling Conflict
Gerry Rauch

The Emotions
Facing Your Feelings
Bert Ghezzi
The Angry Christian
Bert Ghezzi
The Self-Image of a Christian
Mark Kinzer
Living with a Clear Conscience
Mark Kinzer
The Fear Factor
Jim McFadden

Christian Character
Strength under Control
John Keating
How to Become the Person You Were Meant to Be
Peter Williamson
Growing in the Fruit of the Spirit
John Blattner

Personal Relationships
Taming the Tongue
Mark Kinzer

Bert Ghezzi and Peter Williamson
General Editors